Marketing Beyond Your Front Door

Marketing Beyond Your Front Door

by Bob Popyk

Hal Leonard Books
New York

Published in 2009 by Hal Leonard Books
An Imprint of Hal Leonard Corporation
7777 West Bluemound Road
Milwaukee, WI 53213

Trade Book Division Editorial Offices
19 West 21st Street, New York, NY 10010

Printed in the United States of America

Editoral assistant: Laura DeJoseph
Illustrator: Gerry Stockley

Library of Congress Cataloging-in-Publication data is available upon request.

ISBN 978-1-4234-6636-9

www.halleonard.com

Marketing Beyond Your Front Door

Contents

Foreword

Since the first issue of *The Music Trades* appeared in 1890, you could count the outside columnists we've used on one hand. It's not because these people are hard to find. A week doesn't go by without a call or a letter from someone with an idea for a new monthly column. It's just that most of the ideas submitted are either too generic, too insipid, or too dull.

So, 20 years ago, we were thrilled when the opportunity to work with Bob Popyk arose. Bob had wit, style, and a keen understanding of the sales process. To make the proposition even more appealing, he also brought with him a first-hand knowledge of the music industry, gained from years of running his own retail stores.

Each month, Bob has a unique way of blending his own personal experiences, his insights into other industries, and his music industry background into a highly readable and informative column. Along the way, he's built up a strong following of retailers around the world. Subscription renewal forms routinely arrive with "I love Bob's column" scrawled in the margin.

Looking through our archives, we discovered that the last columnist we had before Bob was G.D. Crain, a man our grandfather hired. After a five-year run, Crain stopped writing for *The Music Trades* in 1932 when he left to launch *Advertising Age*, a leading publication for the advertising industry that's still going strong. The roster of *The Music Trades* columnists may be slim, but with G.D. Crain and Bob Popyk, it includes two unique individuals who reflect the quality we try to impart to our work.

We hope you enjoy the following updated collection of columns. More than anything we could say here, they illustrate why Bob Popyk is such a valuable contributor to *The Music Trades*.

Brian T. Majeski, Editor
Paul A. Majeski, Publisher

Author's Note:

I like talking to music retailers and salespeople. My office phone number and e-mail address appears in every one of my columns in *The Music Trades*, so it's easy for people to just pick up the phone or send me a note. And they do. That's where a lot of the material for the columns comes from.

Some dealers like to vent about dealing with the competition, the Internet, the economy, and their employees. Others like to share interesting ideas for getting more customers through the door. Those are the calls and e-mails I like the best. It's great to hear new and interesting ways for getting store personnel involved in bringing more people into the store without spending a lot of cash.

Advertising and promotion are expensive, particularly using major media. It takes a big checkbook, not to mention a crystal ball to know where to spend your money. Participatory activities, lessons, referrals, and personal promotion are much more cost-effective today.

Getting your store salespeople personally involved in finding customers that your competition doesn't know exist is the answer in the years to come. It's not that hard, but dealers have to want to do it. It's easy if you have the right game plan, the right attitude, and the willingness to give new ideas a try.

CHAPTER 1:
Bringing Them Back

The MasterCard Approach to Customer Service

You've seen the commercials: "Baseball tickets: $28. Souvenir program: $8. Hot dog and a soda: $14. An afternoon with your son: Priceless. There are some things money can't buy. For everything else, there's MasterCard." It goes something like that. It seems that we're in a day and age where everything comes down to dollars and cents. And if we can't put a monetary figure on something, we put that thought in print as well. We can talk all we want, offer the greatest savings, and give outstanding customer service, but sometimes if the customer doesn't see it in writing, it's just not the same.

We want to be remembered not only for our great customer service, but for whatever else we can do to ensure that the customers will come back again. And we want those customers to refer us to all of their friends, too. The easiest way to keep them thinking about our "priceless" qualities is to write them down on the invoice or receipt. If you have to sell something below list, write down the regular price on the invoice. Then cross it out and write down the customer's price. If you're including something for free, write that down as well. For example, if you sell a guitar and amp and throw in an extra set of strings and some picks, put those extras on the invoice, list the retail value, then write, "no charge." It's "psychic savings."

There's a car dealer in the Southwest who offers an oil change for $19.95. He does this not only to compete with the Jiffy Lubes and all the other quick-service places, but to bring more customers into his service department. His invoice looks something like this:

Oil Change:	$19.95
Filter:	No charge
Check hoses:	No charge
Check tires:	No charge
Vacuum mats:	No charge
30 minutes or less:	No charge

If his customer watched television in his waiting area, there would probably be a "no charge" notation on the invoice for that, too. Let your customers know you're going out of your way for them. Put your "priceless" qualities in writing.

If you're sitting down with your customers, or they're on the other side of a counter, keep a blank piece of paper close by. Once you start talking about features and benefits and reasons to buy, write them down. If they're on paper, they're more believable.

Maybe you're selling a piano. Your customers are next to you at your desk. They've already seen a couple of different brands at other dealers. It's down to your model and dollars and cents. Don't just give them a price and wait for an answer. Write down the tag price on a piece of paper where they can watch. List some major features. Cross out the first price, then write the price you want them to pay. Show them how much they'll save. Circle that number. Now those savings are real to them because they're on paper.

Sincerity is another "priceless" factor. You may not write "Sincerity: No Charge" on an invoice, but there are other ways to demonstrate it. For example, do you always thank your customers? A while back, I was in a supermarket where my $100-worth of groceries was being rung up by a teenaged, gum-chewing young lady busily preoccupied with making a lot of small talk with the tattooed jock doing the bagging. A few times I caught her ringing up the same things twice. She was a little put off with me interfering with her social life, and once our transaction was complete, she gave me my change and went back to chatting. I turned and said, "You didn't say thank you." She said, "It's on the receipt."

That was one case when having something written down didn't make me feel like a valued customer. This is probably an extreme example. I'm sure you say thank you when you make a sale. It's only common sense. But you might consider also writing, "Thank you!" in longhand and signing your name on the receipt. When the customer finds that you actually wrote "Thank you!" and signed your name below it, it's a really nice touch. That personal attention to your customer is "priceless."

Let your customers know when you go out of your way for them. Showing them is one thing. Telling them about it is another. But listing it as part of the sale at "no charge" will be a benefit to both of you. They'll feel good about it, and you'll have a better chance of not only bringing them back in again, but also of having them refer you to their friends.

Clever Is as Clever Does

I don't get involved with buying office supplies for my company—one of our staff handles it. Unbeknownst to me, we had changed suppliers over the past couple of months and were no longer doing business with a local company. A young woman from the office supply place used to call on us for orders, until someone in my company made an executive decision to go elsewhere, perhaps because of lower prices, bigger catalog selection, better delivery ... I'm not sure. But I did find out that the salesperson was not getting anywhere with the person on our staff doing the buying. She was up against a brick wall. No orders. No biz. Think about what you would do in the same situation if you were the salesperson. Would you just give up? Try to hack your prices so you could compete?

Personality skills, creativeness, and cleverness do pay off when you are trying to put a sale together. They are also essential for repeat business. In this case, it came by way of an envelope in the mail ... to me. In the envelope was an article about my book *Here's My Card*, and it was laminated. There was also a card with a handwritten note. Here is the note, word for word:

"Bob, Congratulations on your book! It looks very interesting. I'm looking forward to reading it. We miss doing business with your company and would love the opportunity to earn your business back. Thought that I might be able to "buy" a little of your time. Sincerely, Nicole Neri."

Included with the article and the note was her business card *laminated* to a dollar bill. I set the whole thing aside on my desk. At the end of the day I didn't know what to do with the card and the dollar. Throw it away? C'mon, it's a buck. I can't do that. Should I try to separate the card from the dollar with a razor blade? It would take too long, and besides, my time is worth more. I left it there until morning.

I came in the next day, sat at my desk, and there was this stupid business card-laminated-to-a-dollar thing. At that point, I went to the person in our office in charge of office supplies and said: "Let's order a laminating machine from this person ... I want to do the same thing." And we did. We are now doing business with this company again, and we've been laminating our business cards to just about anything to create more interest in our company, our books, and our publications ever since.

You see, you never know where the next creative sales idea is going to come from. It could be from a business down the street, your competition, someone on your staff, or just from letting your mind float while you're in the shower. But when a sale starts to fall through the cracks, or a customer starts to look elsewhere, there's a way to keep it from happening. Maybe it's just an issue of getting the customer back to see you one more time. Or getting them to call you on the phone. Or just getting them to like you a little more.

More sales are lost through lack of communication than any other reason. And if you can't get your customer to open up to you and talk to you and tell you what the problem is, you could be spinning your wheels. That's where a little creativeness and cleverness comes into play. They don't teach it in school—you have to learn it on your own. Years ago we could "hard sell" a customer into buying. Today's customers know the tricks and the closes; they don't want to be sold, they want to buy.

So the next time a customer says "I can buy it cheaper on the Internet," "there are better deals down the street," or "I'd rather buy something used" or whatever, don't give up. It's better to think about what it would take to get the customer to like *you* a little bit more, then your product. And a little cleverness along the way could be the answer.

Customer Service = Customer Retention: True or False?

My dry cleaner has a very large picture framed in his store. It shows several men in white shirts and ties, but without pants. The men are playing miniature golf in front of a dry cleaner's shop with a sign that reads, "Play Golf Free While Having Your Suit Pressed." The caption on the picture reads "Great customer service can beat the pants off the competition." There's a lot of truth to that statement. This past week I had two unbelievably bad experiences with companies I have done business with for years. I will probably never return to the one store simply because of an uncaring attitude. The other—whom I swore I would never do business with again—got me to change my mind.

The first was a car dealer. It was a Buick dealership where I had purchased and serviced at least four of my cars. I dropped my car off for service one night. The car was supposed to receive a simple inspection, oil, lube and filter. Nothing out of the ordinary. They left a message for me the next day saying to call them, as they couldn't fit my car in because they were too busy. I would have to wait at least four days for an inspection, and none of their bays were available for an oil change. So I gave them a call. I asked for the service department. After five minutes on hold, I hung up and called back. I asked for service again.

This time I got the body shop. They said they couldn't transfer the call, and to call back. I called back again. After another five minutes on hold, I hung up and called once more—same ordeal. So this time I called back and asked for the manager. He wasn't available. I asked to talk with a salesperson. One of the salespeople picked up the phone, and I asked him to go to the service department and find someone who would talk to me. I explained I had been on hold previously for 15 minutes while calling back three times. He reluctantly did what I asked, and after a little more time on hold, a person in service picked up. He said he realized that I had dropped off my car on Thursday, but they couldn't get to it for at least four days. They were too busy. I explained the inspection tag had expired and I needed it quickly. He said, "That's the way it is."

When I mentioned the problems I had getting through, I was told that I was calling after 4 p.m.—when inexperienced people answer the phones, and when the service department has too much to do. He asked if I wanted to bring the car back on the following Wednesday or Thursday. I said I would "put him on hold for a minute" while I called the Buick dealer across town. They said I could bring it in right away. That service department said they didn't want me driving with an expired inspection sticker, and they always do oil changes in 30 minutes. I said I would be right over. I then went back to the person on hold and told him to forget it. I didn't need the aggravation. I decided that my next car probably won't come from that dealership. I called the next day and explained the situation to a salesperson. "Things just aren't the same since the old manager left," she said. "We're having these complaints all the time, and we have to bring in temps to answer the phone."

My second customer service run-in happened with a golf equipment catalogue source. It's a company where I have purchased putters, drivers, wedges, golf bags, and golf balls with the unrealistic expectation of bringing my game to a better level. I had placed an order for some Nike logo golf balls. I was told, when placing the order, that they would arrive in four to six weeks. My credit card was charged, yet they never arrived. I called them after six weeks and was told I ordered six dozen and the minimum order was 12 dozen, so they wouldn't be coming. I asked why they never called to inform me. The customer representative said, "I guess we were too busy." But he was willing to give me 13 dozen for the price of 12. I said I didn't want them that bad, and to send me a check back, since I had used a debit card. He explained he couldn't do that, but that he would get back to me. It was not their place to make sure items were shipped. The customers are responsible to let them know if a problem occurs.

I never got the credit, and I never got a refund. So I called back and asked to talk with a principal of the company. Believe it or not, I had a VP on the phone in seconds. I told him what he could do with his company, his catalog, and his golf balls, and he said he couldn't believe this had happened to me. He said he was going to call Nike and call me right back. When he called back he offered to give me seven dozen balls for the price of six, have my last name imprinted on the balls (like Tiger Woods), and ship them over-

night at no extra cost. He told me to call him directly with any future problems I may incur with his company. I liked this guy. I told him I had already destroyed his catalogue and had asked to be taken of the mailing list. He said he would send me two more, keep me on the list, and asked that I please continue to use his company. Plus, a gift would be coming to me in the mail because of the inconvenience.

What a difference his attitude made. I now tell my golfing buddies about the company's great customer service, and I'm getting ready to place an order for a $300 driver—that I don't need. It's guaranteed to take five strokes off my game.

Do you see the difference? Customer retention was important to one while the other dealership had too many other things to think about, beside customers. The dealer had a change in manager, change in people handling incoming calls, and too much service work. This was not my problem; my problem was my car. They are going to find out quickly that there are other dealers who do 30-minute oil changes, look out for their customers, and sell cars as well. They're also able to answer their phones without putting customers on hold for five minutes at a time.

The golf retailer knew that golfers can be impulsive buyers. They will purchase items they don't need, for twice the price they should pay, and on a regular basis. Be nice to them—that's all it takes. Customer retention is how your business is going to grow. You decide how important it is. Remember, customer service is an action, not a department.

E-Mail v. Direct Mail:
Which Reaches Your Customers Better?

Not so long ago, only a few people had e-mail addresses. Now, no self-respecting computer owner (and that's just about everybody) would be without one. Just as very few people today are without a cell phone, cable TV, Internet access, and e-mail.

Sure, a small number of people still have rotary phones, but even these folks can have an e-mail account. In fact, just about every age group has e-mail. Five-year-olds have it, as well as 95-year-olds. E-mail is cheap. You can send out letters to your e-mail list as many times as you want without huge postage costs. Since e-mail has little cost and direct mail rates are high, it came as a surprise to me to find out many music store retailers are planning to increase spending on direct mail.

I spoke with a dozen retailers over the past few months regarding how well their e-mail list performs against their direct mail programs. I found out that for getting new business (or more business), direct mail has been producing better results. I didn't understand why.

Just a few years ago, many music retailers abandoned direct mail almost overnight in favor of e-mail and websites. There seemed to be a massive migration toward electronic marketing because everybody was doing it and nobody wanted to seem "out of step." E-mail "blasting" could reach tens of thousands of buyers at a fraction of the cost of direct mail. And it was quick and easy to implement. But I think, since everybody was doing it, it wasn't taken as seriously as direct mail. Constant bombardment from tens (if not hundreds) of thousands of spam operations was too much for many customers to bear. E-mail started to be intrusive. Today you have to compete with Nigerian money scams, Viagra at give-away prices, stock hypes, porn sites, and prescription drug mail order firms. You also have to compete with e-mail solicitations from big companies like Pier 1, Best Buy, Circuit City, Amazon, and so on down the list.

Here are some of the reasons that I was given from music retailers who are going back to direct mail marketing on a regular basis. First of all, everyone takes direct mail seriously. When the mail arrives, it's one of the most important moments of the day, both at the office and at home. We complain if it's late (at least we do at our office) and feel deprived if there is nothing of any importance. Usually we stop whatever we're doing when the "snail mail" arrives to go through it. In other words, we still view postal mail as a priority. Don't you feel slighted when you find out there's nothing in your morning mail at home? It's not exactly the same for e-mail.

Second, postal mail has a more personal feel to it. If your name is on it, it's yours. I would much rather receive a Hallmark card in the mail than an electronic greeting card. Most people feel that way. It just isn't the same. More thought and effort goes into sending a card in the mail. We give the most attention to the mail that seems the most personal. We reject the mail that looks like nothing more than an ad. With direct mail, you can easily personalize the envelope, letter, or marketing copy.

Third, regular mail is tangible. You can hold it in your hand. You can feel it. You can toss it in the trash if it's something you don't want, but it takes more than a click to get rid of it. I know of people who hang on to direct mail response cards for months before they send them in. E-mail is designed for instant action, and most of the time it's instant deletion. That's not to say that an e-mail list and e-mail letters don't work. It's just that direct mail seems to work better, in spite of the cost. Sure, you can do both, but an aggressive, well-thought-out direct mail campaign still seems to bring in more immediate bucks.

I remember years back, having an in-store concert and clinic on a date that kind of snuck up on me. We forgot to promote it until just a week before. While we were running around trying to figure out what to do, we decided to send out a thousand-piece mailer as well as get our salespeople on the phone with our past customers and try to get them in. In the midst of the confusion, half of the direct mail envelopes were sent out unstuffed by mistake. There was nothing in them. And half of those people who received the empty envelope called to ask what was in them. We told the people about the concert and clinic, and many of those people came and brought their friends. Compare that to e-mail. Send an e-mail to someone with no subject line or no message, and it gets deleted in a flash. Forget who it came from. It becomes one less thing to deal with. Besides, spam filters are grabbing a lot of the messages, even the ones sent to your opt-in list.

So, don't throw away your customer mailing list in favor of an e-mail list. Continue to update it. Buy a good mailing list once in a while to attract new business. You should continue to use your e-mail list, but don't forget about direct mail. It still has tremendous benefits.

Staying in Touch Will Get You More Business (and Better Gross)

Most people will probably never get to meet Sam Price. And that's too bad. Sam Price is probably one of the best salespeople this country has. He's not in the *Guinness World Records* book, and you probably won't read about him in *Time* magazine. He doesn't write books or give seminars. He doesn't sell instruments. I don't even know if he knows anything about the music business. You see, Sam Price sells cars. To be more exact, Sam sells Chevrolets for Al Serra Chevrolet in the little town of Grand Blanc, Michigan.

Sam doesn't own a cellular phone. He doesn't have a laptop computer or a fax machine. Sam says that all he needs is a comfortable pair of shoes that don't hurt his feet, so he can walk his customers up and down all those rows of new and used cars. Sometimes he's on his feet for 12 hours a day.

In one year, Sam sold 323 cars. That's a lot of metal over the curb—a lot of names on the dotted line. As a matter of fact, to do it he had to get about 1,300 names on the dotted line, because about three out of four of his deals never pan out. Three out of four of his customers are credit rejects, or else they suffer from buyer's remorse, can't come up with the money, decide to look around more, or simply decide to keep what they have.

And yet, Sam still delivers about 27 cars a month, which is about twice what the average car salesperson sells. What makes this so amazing is the fact that Sam Price works at a one-price dealership. There's no haggling. There's no negotiating. You pay what's on the window or you don't buy the car. His dealership changed over to this program a few years ago. And

when it did, Sam was scared stiff. He didn't know what to think. Sam had been the master of the hard sell. He was used to pressure tactics and psychological manipulation. Common to his daily life was a long string of "If I could ... , would ya ... ?" questions.

In 1991, he sold 270 cars by doing everything he could to make the customer sign immediately. He would use every close in the book, and if that didn't work, he'd bring in the super-closer from the back room to work them over one more time. He figured if they walked away without buying, he'd never see them again.

Then one day, the entire scene changed. His dealership adopted a one-price program for selling cars. Overnight, all the slam-dunk skills he had honed became passé. In their place was a new system of relationship marketing that stressed a quality image and product reliability beyond reproach.

Sam didn't know if he could handle the change. But he made the adjustment—and it wasn't easy.

How would you react if you were used to wheeling and dealing prices all day, and all of a sudden you had to stick to list or whatever the tag says? Are you a dealer who could afford to set a one-price policy and stick to it? If a customer offered you $500 less on a grand piano, would you take it? How about the customer who comes in with a price already from another dealer? If your price is $200 more, would you match it? Or could you shift gears and learn to handle the situation like Sam Price?

Let me tell you about Sam's background. He's one of the nicest people you'll ever talk to, and I've only talked to him on the phone. He was born in 1942, has a wife who's a librarian, a grown son, plus a bachelor's degree in education from the University of Illinois. In his 20s, he played in the backfield with the Miami Dolphins. After that, he ran several Burger King franchises. Then he started selling cars.

It would be almost impossible not to like Sam Price. Talking to him is kind of like talking to Morgan Freeman, star of the movies *Driving Miss Daisy* and *The Shawshank Redemption*. Everything he says makes sense, and he is easy to relate to. Sam's soft-spoken, honest, and in 10 seconds, you know he wants to be your friend. He doesn't fit the stereotype of the slick, fast-talking used car salesman. Sam's like someone you'd like living next door to you.

Sam says that it is the only way you can maintain your gross without cutting the price. With one price, you have to sell yourself and you have to sell the dealership, he says. In the past, when it all came down to a couple of hundred bucks either way, it didn't matter if the customer liked you or not. Now it matters a whole lot. The customer has to trust you. Instead of feeling he beat you up for the lowest price, he has to feel it's a fair price.

Sam says that, if you're going to stick to one price, you have to really understand a customer's needs. Sometimes customers confuse their wants with their needs, so they come in wanting a Corvette, but what they really need is a Blazer. Find the real need and fill it. And if you're going to sell at one price, Sam says, you have to give the customer breathing room. You've got to know when to back off. In fact, Sam doesn't even go with his customer on a test drive. He doesn't want the prospect to feel pressured.

"Too many pitches and you start to oversell," Sam says. "Customers have to make up their own minds."

The trick to Sam Price's technique is this: there isn't one. Selling at one price takes total commitment, Sam says. First and foremost, you have to be willing to put in the time.

Sam also says that he hands over the keys personally every time he delivers a car. He says that a car is a major purchase, and he doesn't want a stranger getting involved in his sale. And once you buy a car from Sam, he remembers you forever, so you remember him when you're ready for another car. He keeps in touch with every customer as a friend, because friends refer friends.

Think about Sam's philosophy in your music business. If a customer comes in and wants an acoustic piano, but really needs a digital piano with recording abilities, are you going to try to separate the two? If your customer asks about a $20,000 grand piano, but has a $10,000 buying budget, do you really spend the time analyzing her needs? Do you write up a sale and forget about the customer as soon as he or she leaves your store? Do you take a few minutes to find out a few things about your customers, like what you might have in common, so it's easier to become their friend? When you sell an instrument, do you write "Thank You" on the sales slip and sign your name? Do you tell your customers to call you personally if there's a problem, so you can handle it yourself to make sure that it gets resolved?

Sam says he doesn't worry about being number one. The only thing you can control is your own attitude. If you're afraid of rejection, it will hold you back. If you think you have to discount to make a sale, you become a prophet of your own destiny, he says. Fifty different closes aren't going to work any more. Customers object to something that isn't right for them. My job is to find something that is right for them.

So the next time your customers say they can save $1,000 down the street, or they can buy it near wholesale somewhere else, think about Sam Price. He sells at one price, while his competition haggles, negotiates, and wheels and deals. And he sells twice what they do.

Go figure.

CHAPTER 2:
Taking Care of Business

Do You Provide a "Hang Out" for Your Customers?

Years ago, when I was growing up, I loved to hang out in music stores. In fact, I still do. I remember Grinnell's in Detroit, Auburn Music in upstate New York, and Manny's in New York City. It was a kick just to look at and try new instruments, talk music with the salespeople, and meet fellow musicians. I remember that, in the old days, so many musicians hung around Sam Ash Music in New York that people would call there to book a band. When I built my last two retail music stores I put in fireplaces (with chairs and a couch) for people who came in and wanted to warm up during the six months of winter our area of the country has, and just visit and chat about music and instruments and hang out in front of the fire.

Instead of thinking "outside the box" on ways to create more revenue, maybe we should just keep thinking "inside the box" and concentrate on the customers who are already coming in our store. Maybe we can find out who their friends are and get them to come in as well. Possibly the parents who drop off their kids for music lessons, scoot down the street and pick them up an hour later would come in and maybe buy something if you provide the right amenities. I'm not just talking about a waiting area outside the studios with last year's magazines and a TV. I mean a nice place to hang out, talk music, look at instruments, get a cup of coffee, and spend some pleasant time.

I heard about Beacock Music in Vancouver, Washington, a music store owned by Gail and Russell Beacock. Beacock Music was founded in 1976, and is a full-line retail music store specializing in music education. I learned that they are the largest independent music store in the Pacific Northwest. In addition to retailing a wide selection of band instruments, sheet music, guitars, pro-audio, keyboards, and percussion, they also have a full service repair shop and an online store. I also heard that they have an actual coffee shop in their store.

Washington State is a little far for me to visit, so I gave them a call. Neither Gail nor Russel was there, but I talked with Keith Dwiggins, their assistant manager of sales. It was fun talking with Keith on the phone. He told me that they have a "little Starbucks" area, with a counter, a nook with stools, and other places for people to sit. The staff who takes care of the sheet music department are also the food handlers. They have coffee, soda, and other beverages, as well as bagels, pastries, and soups.

Keith told me, for a store to do this right, you need the space and the personnel to man this type of thing. The coffee shop entices parents to stay while their kids are taking lessons, and for musicians to come in off the street and just "hang out." And get this one—the coffee shop also turns a profit.

I know quite a few piano and organ stores that offer kind of a "community area" with puzzles and other activities. Some have fish tanks and cable TV. Some offer Wi-Fi. Piano and Organ Distributors in Clay, New York, have live birds in cages chirping all day.

So while other dealers are doing the "thinking outside the box" thing, maybe now is a good time to go back to what made retail music stores successful dozens of years ago … way back before catalogs, e-Bay, and Internet sites. It was less of a commodity sale and "who has the lowest price" thing. It was more of a comfortable atmosphere where you got to talk to your friends. And those friends were the salespeople at the music store. They demonstrated, suggested, and sold, while just making conversation. Those customers brought in their friends to do the same.

Sometimes we need to just get back inside the box. What's the potential return if you significantly improve your delivery of core customer wants and needs? What if you come up with a better way of solving customers' everyday problems, instead of just coming up with something new? Those problems might start with what to do while the kids take lessons. Or maybe just a nicer experience while visiting your store. Or simply, just a great place to "hang out." More sales starts with more customer traffic, and you might not have to come up with a whole new bag of tricks to get more people in your store. A nice place to sit down and have a cup of coffee, while trying out an instrument and talking about a purchase, could do it.

The Magic Is in the Mix

I talked with a dealer the other day who has had (what he terms) "excellent results" selling products on his website. You can run your whole business through one great website. Rents decrease because you can cut back on existing floor space, you won't need huge inventory displays, and you won't need all the salespeople. You can do it all online. "Click here to order." "Click here for more information." You can even get rid of your toll-free number. This dealer says it won't be long until he can close his doors altogether and run the whole operation from his laptop.

I know e-commerce is hot. You read about it in magazines, hear about it on the radio, see the crazy commercials on TV, and watch the dot-com stocks react like they're on a trampoline. It's big business. At least bigger than ever before.

But get this one. The Society of Consumer Affairs Professionals in Business (SOCAP) released a survey of almost 6,000 Americans aged 18 and over to find out how folks respond when actually placing orders. The survey asked whether they preferred to buy online or through an toll-free number. Guess what? Most people listed the toll-free number as their first choice. E-mail was second, and web-based service was third. But here's another interesting little statistic from Ernst and Young: 50% of corporate websites *don't list a toll-free number.*

When some of these businesses were asked why they didn't have a toll-free number, many said it was because they only wanted to take orders or do business on the phone during "normal business hours." But whether you're selling to the better part of North America or even just to your hometown, what are "normal hours" anyway? *Your* hours? Your customers' hours? There's no easy answer. At some point, you're going to need a way to process inquiries and sales during the better part of the day or night. It's going to take toll-free numbers and online ordering, together with expanded customer service. And if you don't offer them, your competition will.

Still think an accelerated e-commerce program—all by itself—will be the answer? It seems to be the hottest thing. Sure, it's attractive. Just think how much you could save without:

- Direct mail campaigns
- Yellow page advertising
- Newspaper advertising
- All the telephone lines

But also think how much you could lose without them.

Consider it carefully. Stand-alone e-business may be just wishful think-ing. Scientist and author Lewis Thomas said: "Most scientific hypotheses, including what seem the brightest and the best, turn out to be wrong." Take a look in the papers. It is hard to pick up *The Wall Street Journal* without seeing an e-business going down in flames. Everyone hears the stories about how cheaply you can buy products online. Now we're hearing the stories about many e-commerce sites not raising enough cash to keep themselves in business—few businesses can make it without showing a profit. All kinds of e-whatevers—pet, toy, and food sites that just thought they could make it exclusively online.

And therein lies the answer to sales and marketing strategies in the 21st century. The magic is going to be in a combination of response venues, not just one specific thing. No matter what you might believe, the future is not going to be all online. It's not just a better website, dazzling graphics and a "click here to order" or click "for more information" or a click "to be contacted" button. It would be nice, but it's not going to happen.

On the other side of the coin, don't ignore the importance of web-based business. If your store is not in some way involved in e-commerce, you're probably shortchanging yourself as well. It takes several strategies to keep up. Today, few businesses can make it with just one type of promotional effort or sales program. If you don't have a website, get one. If you're not doing direct mail, start. If you're not using major media for advertising, consider it. Today, it is very rare that anything works by itself.

The same goes for response venues. With a toll-free number, a customer can get instant customer service satisfaction. E-mail sites, like Amazon. com, get back to customers later that day. US Airways says that you will hear back in "five to seven days." Customers need to have an option. No options can result in no business.

So, it seems the answer for most businesses will be a well-thought-out ad budget, a great website, a toll-free number, unparalleled customer service, personal promotion (with business cards of course), some direct-mail campaigns, quality customer relationships, and a good business plan. You're also going to need a good lawyer and a good accountant. Just a good website alone is not going to get you orders "out the whazoo." (Remember that commercial during the Super Bowl … the one where the guy had so much web business coming "out the whazoo" that he needed surgery? Yeah, that one. Can't think of the name of the company, can you?) The magic is in the mix. Don't put all your faith—or money—in one single selling strategy. You're going to need several. Find the ones that are really working for you and capitalize on them. And stay on top of it. Track your results. If you just lean back in your chair with your feet up, you'll be falling backwards before you know it.

The 10 Greatest Salespeople You Never Knew

I've been connected with the retail music industry for almost 40 years. I've had the chance to know industry veterans like Karl Bruhn, Larry Linkin, and Bob Fletcher before they retired, and I got to meet industry legends like Bill Schultz, Vic Firth, and John D'Addario, who are still involved today. And along the way I've met some people who shouldn't have been in the industry at all (the soap lady at Baldwin Piano instantly comes to mind). One of the nicest parts about the music industry is that once you're in it, it's very difficult to get out. It becomes a part of your life. It's a really fun business to be in.

The music industry has also enjoyed the talents of some pretty dynamic salespeople. Over the years, I took note of some of the outstanding people, and why they were so good at sales. I learned a lot from them. So, as a committee of one, I made up a list of who I think the best retail music industry salespeople from the past few decades are. Some of them you might know; some of them you probably never heard of. Most are not household names. If you never had the opportunity to meet them, you missed a lot. Here are my votes for the top 10:

1) **George Vigorito**—George Vigorito sold phonographs at the Wurlitzer store on Wabash in downtown Chicago just after World War II. He was an attorney by trade, but ended up becoming head of sales for the Wurlitzer Company in DeKalb, Illinois, during its heyday. George always said: "Find out what type of music the customers like to play or listen to, then demo the instrument only using that type of music." George was outgoing, assertive, and could get your attention like nobody you've ever seen.

2) **John Phanco**—John Phanco was also at Wurlitzer. He had a territory, and was then made sales manager. He could sell a piano or organ in minutes, because he was so likeable. He always said: "Get the customer to like you, and they will trust you. If they trust you, they will buy from you." John was a clever guy. Another one of his bits of wisdom was: "When you're at the store, answer the phone breathless; sound like you're busy, but you're making time to talk on the phone just for them." You would have liked John.

3) **Bob Tackett**—Bob Tackett sat at the right hand of Vern Schafer at Colton Piano & Organ in Southern California during the days when Colton's sold organs and pianos by the hundreds. Bob always said: "We're not looking for one way to sell 100 pianos, we're looking for 100 ways to sell one piano." He was an interesting, aggressive, charming person. And he was always

anxious to learn. He died way too early.

4) Bud Streep—Bud Streep was a former President of NAMM, and the owner of Streep Music in Orlando, Florida. Bud believed in community involvement. Before Ticketron, you could go to Streep Music to buy tickets to concerts and other local events at his "community box office." He believed in getting people through the door any way that he could, and it started with high visibility in the community.

5) Evelyn Terrell—Evelyn Terrell was a legend. She had her own system for class lessons that the Conn Organ Company ended up adopting. In her own stores, she sold console organs like most stores sold guitar picks. She knew the name of every one of the hundreds and hundreds of students, and had a sixth sense for knowing a lot about each person. Everyone liked her, and when she said, "You should buy this one here," they did. She made selling simple.

6) Stan Lischner—Stanley Lischner worked for the Sorkin Music Company, a musical instrument distributor. His dealers called him "Stanley from Sorkin." It was years before I even knew his last name. He would express concern when a dealer would say "business is slow," or "the economy is bad," or "nobody is coming in." He never let a negative dealer bother him. Stanley would offer a ton of advice on what to do when business slowed down, while other reps just gave up and went home. Dealers would place an order with Stanley because they knew he had a genuine interest in their business.

7) Frances Jones—Frances Jones was the first female board member of NAMM. She was the former head of Jordan-Kitts Music in Washington, DC, and died recently at the age of 95. "Miss Jones," as she was known, had incredible networking skills and believed that it was "*who* you know as much as *what* you know." She earned an unprecedented amount of respect from her customers and from the manufacturers that Jordan-Kitts represented. She had a talent for getting to know everybody.

8) Don Wennlund—Don Wennlund was with the Lowrey Organ Company in Joliet, Illinois. He would talk to anybody—he didn't care who you were. And everybody would listen; it was a gift. I'm sure he never had a boring day in his life. When you have a genuine interest in somebody and it shows, selling seems to come easier. He made selling a no-brainer. One of his favorite phrases was, "I'm here to bring culture to Joliet." Will Rogers would have bought an organ from him.

9) Fritz Newell—I really liked Fritz Newell. I knew him when he worked for Fletcher Music. His friends called him "the big elf." He was probably around 6'4" and looked like someone who could wrestle for the WWF. His talent was in knowing when to stop talking. A customer would say, "I want to go home and think about it," and he would say absolutely nothing. He would just keep looking at them. Next thing you knew they would be pulling out a check and saying, "How much do you need now?" Fritz always said: "Know when to stop talking. Know when to listen."

10) Maurice H. Berlin—M.H. Berlin, as he was known, was founder of Chicago Music. He spearheaded the acquisition of F.E. Olds, Story & Clark, Gibson, Reynolds, and Lowrey. He had an uncanny sense of knowing which would be the right product, at the right time, at the right price. He also thought that selling was a partnering process. Selling should be a "win-win situation." When Chuck Levin's store burned down during the riots in DC, he helped put Washington Music back in business by getting them guitars, and waiting for payment until they were sold. He was a keen believer in relationship selling—holding your customer's hand when necessary. It worked then; it works today.

I'm sure there were people I didn't know, and some I forgot. But these are the 10 who stick in my mind to this day. They provided some great lessons. They were great people. And I'm always looking for someone else I can learn something from.

10 More Great Music Industry Salespeople

Several years ago I wrote a column about the 10 greatest salespeople you never knew. They were music-industry veterans who had passed away. The first list included George Vigorito, John Phanco, Fritz Newell, Bob Tackett, Stanley Lischner, Evelyn Terrell, Don Wennlund, M.H. Berlin, Bud Streep and Frances Jones. A few months ago, I mentioned I was putting together an updated list of another 10, and was looking for nominations. I received many. The only criteria were that they had to be good salespeople, well-liked individuals, and deceased. So, as a committee of one, here are the picks for this year's 10 greatest salespeople the world may not have known:

1) **John Yousling**—A lot of people including Scotty Anderson nominated John who was from Wurlitzer. I knew John personally. He kind of looked like Andy Gump (if you go back that far). I don't mean it in a bad way. He had a nonthreatening, likeable demeanor, and could sell someone without them knowing they were being sold. He knew the Wurlitzer instruments inside out; he helped make the Hobby Lesson Course an integral part of the sales process. He helped dealers get higher margins by teaching features and benefits. He had a raft of information, but never let it get in the way. He was a genuinely nice person.

2) **Wilbur Marker**—He was nominated by Harry Carter, the former owner of Sorden Music Co. in Iowa. Harry said that Wilbur Marker was a sales rep for CMI, who sold Olds band instruments and Gibson guitars. Wilbur worked without an order book. He always scheduled his calls at the convenience of his dealers, not his convenience, and always came prepared to help. He made you feel like you weren't being pushed into buying, but were buying sensibly for the season you were in at the time. Most of all, Wilbur Marker was a gentleman, with the emphasis on "gentle."

3) **Josef Friedman**—A Curtis-trained percussionist, at one time Josef taught at Wurlitzer in Philadelphia. Along the way he was a sales manager at Thomas Organ. Later he was sales rep calling primarily on wholesalers, representing lines such as Mari strings and Remo. Josef had the unique ability to say "yes" to any question. Whatever you needed, he would get it, or would do it for you. Gerson Rosenbloom of Medley Music in Bryn Mawr, Pennsylvania, said that Josef was a continual student of selling, and constantly went to the NAMM seminars, even though he could probably teach many of the classes. Gerson said Josef was "one of the sweetest human beings the music industry ever had".

4) **Nick Orlando**—This will come as a shock to readers, because many people didn't realize Nick passed away in October 2005. Dennis Houlihan

of Roland is among the many people who praised Nick. Nick Orlando was a longtime keyboard sales executive who started Technics Musical Instruments. He enjoyed two successful careers, first with Wurlitzer's retail operation, and then Thomas Organs before the Technics opportunity was presented to him. When most of his contemporaries were planning their retirement, Nick got back into the game, and in a relatively short time fashioned the Technics brand into then one of the most respected names in the home keyboard business. Nick was a class act.

5) Jim Stanton—Art Olson from Artistic Pianos in San Marcos, California, nominated Jim. I would have too. Jim worked as a piano salesperson for Guido Singer at Clark Music in Syracuse, New York. Man, what a sales guy. Nobody was safe from Jim. He sold pianos and organs to the mailman, the teachers, the UPS driver, and anybody who would hold still long enough to listen. Once there was a fire at the store next door that butted up against their building. Smoke and water was all over the place. Firemen were running through the store to make sure everything was out, and Jim stopped one of the firemen, and lifted up a tarp to show him a console piano. He showed him there was hardly any damage and the fireman could buy it at a heck of a discount. Next thing you know he was writing up a contract.

Jim would regularly take trips up to northern New York State alone in his car with a bunch of brochures, and call on piano and organ teachers in the small towns. He always came back with a couple of sales invoices, even though the teachers never saw the instrument they bought until it was delivered. Even though Jim sold a ton of pianos and organs, he couldn't play a note. People bought because of him. It's not that Jim was slick, but he had a believable personality. He told people what they wanted to hear. I remember Jim was also a whiz at liar's poker. Of course, nobody could beat him. People just took what he said as gospel. Everybody liked Jim; I liked Jim. May he rest in peace.

6) Jack Scott—Bob Tringali, Bob Zadel, Bob Carbone, and dozens of other people nominated Jack. I first met Jack when he was with Conn Organ, before he became VP of Samick pianos. Of all the stories and incidents I remember about Jack, I recall when I was a dealer and Jack was helping us work a State Fair. He was showing a customer a Conn Organ that wholesaled for about $1,200. It was after the Fair closed and people were leaving, but Jack had held onto the customer. I wanted to leave too. The organ was tagged at $2,595, and the customer offered $2,200. I motioned to Jack to take it, and he motioned to me to get the heck away. He sold it for full tilt. Jack was a unique individual, a really good guy, and had terrific sales ability. I liked Jack. We were friends.

7) Wayne Mitchell—I didn't know Wayne, but I found out that half the industry did. Bob Jones of Samick Music said that Wayne Mitchell started Organ Center in Hollywood, then put a deal together with Joe Benaron who had the rights to the Vox instruments before The Beatles made Vox famous. He started the Vox Guitar Center, which in turn became Guitar Center. Wayne started in the automobile business, but found the margins were better with musical instruments. He always said that "gross margins mean nothing, but gross profits mean everything." Larry Thomas and Marty Albertson worked for Wayne Mitchell. He had an incredible sense for running a business. Wayne was ahead of his time.

8) Chuck Hale—Chuck owned Hale Piano and Organ in Florida. Their motto was, "If you want a piano, go to Hale". There wouldn't be enough room in this column to list all the people who nominated Chuck. He had Hammond, Steinway, and Yamaha franchises in the incredible growth years in Fort Lauderdale. I don't think anyone ever mentioned a harsh word about Chuck, even his competitors. He was a good golfer, a good salesperson, and a fine human being.

9) Don Leslie—Don is my own choice and inventor of the Leslie Speaker. Through the years a lot of companies tried to take it away from him. No one ever succeeded. He was low-key, very inventive, and knew what it took to sell his product. He should be in the music-industry Hall of Fame.

10) Vito Pascucci—Vito repaired instruments for Glenn Miller during World War II and then became CEO of Leblanc, a company he built. Vito was a tireless seller of music and the many benefits from participating in the school band and orchestra. After his death, the company was never the same again. He would always return his calls, and would always listen to dealers, even though sometimes he didn't agree with them. He was an industry icon and legend. Truly a giant of his time.

It's sad that these people are no longer with us, but I'm glad their memories live on. The friends you make in the music industry are your friends for life. Nobody gets out alive. We seem to stay in it forever.

And I think that's just great.

"It's the Economy, Stupid."

I've had more than the usual amount of phone calls, e-mail, regular mail, and impromptu conversations the past few months regarding business being just a little slow. To some it seems to be even worse, and I've been hearing from those who are very concerned that it might be awhile until it gets better. I always ask why are sales off?

Here are the top 10 reasons people give me when they tell me why business has been slow for them:

1) We still haven't recovered from 9/11.
2) The war in Iraq
3) The stock market is in the toilet.
4) People just don't want to spend money.
5) Customers' credit cards are maxed out and they are heavily in debt.
6) A lot of people were laid off.
7) We are in a recession.
8) The Bush administration is to blame.
9) People don't want what we sell any more.
10) It's the economy, stupid.

OK. I always feel I've been enlightened when they give me the reasons for not writing sales, so when they ask me for suggestions, I have only two:

1) Do something about it.
2) Quit.

Now, assuming they want to stay in their present line of work, the only other option is to do something about it. How about you? Do you have a plan of attack when business slows down? Or do you just do the same thing day after day until business gets better? Maybe you have all the sales and business you want, but with a little creativity and assertiveness you could have even more. And when things slow down, your well will never run dry.

Here are some ideas that you can use right away to get more business. There is no magic bullet, but if you think outside the box, just one idea put to use could increase your business tremendously. They are not easy to implement, but then again, no one said selling is easy all the time. (Selling is the highest paid hard work, and the lowest paid easy work of all the professions). So here are 10 ideas you can try:

1) One day a week, ask everyone you come in contact with if they would like to buy what you sell. Everybody, relatives included. It is a great

exercise. You will be amazed at who will show interest.

2) Take one day a week and write as many thank you notes as you can to customers you've had during the past month. Tell them you'll be giving them a call to see if they know of anyone else who might be interested in what you sell. Do this for a month.

3) Unhook yourself. Take an afternoon to yourself without a computer, cell phone, palm pilot, or any other distraction. Just you with a legal pad and a pen—no radio, no TV, and no people around. Jot down some sales goals, and then write down as many ideas as you can on how you will find more people to talk to, so you can reach your goals. More contacts equal more sales.

4) Go to the library or your local bookstore and get a book on networking. Read it. Make notes to yourself on what would work for you.

5) Call your best customers and tell them you value their opinions. Ask them if they were to go into your business tomorrow, what would they do to get sales? Do they know anybody right now, who would be interested in what you sell? (People love to be asked for advice).

6) "Thinking outside the box" is an old, trite expression, but what can you do differently to increase business? Start by doing some things differently yourself. Wear clothes you normally wouldn't wear; take a different route to work; try foods you don't ordinarily eat; listen to music you seldom listen to; see a movie you wouldn't normally go to; try a different hairstyle. Creative thinking may simply mean the realization that there's no particular virtue in doing things the way they have always been done. And creative thinking can get your brain going, to think of new ways to find more customers

7) Exercise. It's good for you. It's good for your brain. A brisk walk is a good place to start.

8) Find out what brings in customers for other salespeople in town. Talk to other salespeople and see what works for them.

9) What creative advertising methods are working for other businesses in town? What ideas can you use yourself?

10) AND VERY IMPORTANT: Don't tell anyone that business is bad. They won't feel sorry for you; they just won't do business with you. Success breeds success. Act successful, look successful, sound successful, and success will follow.

So next time you think sales are very slow, forget the moaning and complaining. That is just negative energy. Think instead about what you might be able to do to get business back to where you want it.

Are Your Engines Set at "Full Speed Ahead"?

At a past NAMM show in Anaheim, I talked to a lot of dealers who were optimistic about the coming year. Some had a dismal past few months and had already seen a pick-up in business. Others were forecasting a strong spring and summer. However, there were those dealers who said, "As soon as business turns around, I'm going to …" or "We're just waiting for things to get better …"

Well, sometimes it's a long wait. Success isn't the lottery. You can't wait for it to strike. It's not a magical time that finally comes along in the music business. It is not a "destination" thing—it's something you have to work at daily to achieve real success.

Music dealers have to understand that the music business is a compounding cycle of difficulty, adversity, complication, and ups and downs. That is basically how it's destined to be. Some music dealers work it out and continue to grow. Some just don't get it.

When stressed music dealers reach the end of their rope, some try to climb back up, some try to stretch it longer, and some tie a knot and hang on. Others fall off. Few think laterally enough to swing to another rope, but that's sometimes the best answer.

The "other rope" some music dealers choose is to change their business plan, concentrate on different aspects of the music business, take on different lines, look to the web for expanding their market, go after different segments of the music business, distance themselves from their competition, or change careers.

The best "other rope" is simply to choose another way of looking at your current business model, see what's not working, and find a way to fix it. Sometimes that will mean drastic measures must be taken. One thing though is for sure … just waiting for things to get better might be like waiting for your ship to come in while you're at the airport.

We have competition today, like never seen before. There are huge chain stores, mass-market big-box stores, the Internet, discount catalogues, dealers slashing prices in an effort to compete, and low-priced imports coming out of the woodwork. Some dealers are closing up stores, while some are cutting back.

However (and this is a big however), some have rolled with the punches, found different avenues to create revenue, and found unique ways to increase margins. Increasing lesson programs seems to work. Going

after the mature and rec-
reational market is starting
to increase floor traffic and
taking on instruments and
instrument lines that no
one else handles adds to
the bottom line.

If you looked around Anaheim, there were hundreds (if not thousands)
of new music accessory items. No one store can possibly handle them all.
There were lots of impulse and accessory items with big margins. Maybe
it's time to start sifting through these items for a few golden tickets to add
to your inventory.

Many piano dealers told me the past year was rough. Kids have other things
to compete for their interest, such as video games, computers, soccer,
football, baseball, all kinds of other sports, and on and on. The dealer said
storewide clearance sales and college sales weren't pulling as well as in the
past, acoustic piano sales were down, and inventory was piling up.

Could now be time to go after the kids' parents and grandparents instead
of (or as well as) the kids?

Let me share this story. I went to the Home Depot in Ormond Beach,
Florida, a few days ago to buy a piece of carpet to replace a worn-out section in my porch. I already had a type in mind, and I was going to glue it
down to the wood so it wouldn't wrinkle.

I found what I was looking for and went to an attended check-out. (I won't
mention the new self-service check-outs because they scare me.) The clerk
was over-weight, balding, and burly. He looked like an ex-marine, and he
had a tattoo on his forearm that might have been a military insignia at one
time. He probably was in his early 70s. I figured he was part-time. I gave
him the slip for the carpet and realized I had forgotten the glue.

"Damn, I forgot the glue," I said. "It's hell to get old." He said "No, it's a
privilege." I said, "What do you mean?" He answered, "When you get older
you get to do all the fun things you wanted to do in life, and never had time
for. I work here a few days a week because I like dealing with people. I just
bought a Harley-Davidson that I wouldn't have had time to ride before,
and I am also learning to play the piano."

I smiled. He didn't know I'm in the music business, so he probably thought
I was laughing at him because he didn't look like a guy who would take
piano lessons. He said, "Don't think I can play the piano, huh? I probably

have more musical ability than you do. Go get your glue." I figured he didn't buy a $200 keyboard from Wal-Mart, so I asked him what he had for a piano when I returned to his checkout. He told me he paid half the price of his Harley for a decent instrument.

We need to go after these people. There are a lot of recreational musicians out there like this guy who in later years have the time and money to buy instruments and take lessons. We need to swing onto this different rope and go after their friends as well. Or we can keep doing what we're doing and wait until things get better. I hope you do the former, not the latter, because I would hate not seeing you at the Anaheim NAMM show next year.

Increasing Revenue Just Takes the Right Plan

It doesn't take a lot of looking to find businesses that are having a tough time in this period of economic flux. Probably a day doesn't go by without some business owner somewhere saying: "I need more cash," "I need to catch up on my bills," or "I need more sales."

There are a lot of ways to get more money. Some ways take longer than others. If you need a lot of money in a hurry, the quickest way is probably to rob a bank. There seem to be a lot of people doing that right now. In Southern California alone, an average of six banks a day are robbed! That's more than 2,000 bank robberies a year in that area. Nationwide, the numbers have got to be staggering.

Of course, one of the drawbacks of robbing a bank is that it is illegal, and they can put you away for a long time if you get caught. Now, just for a minute, let's think about what steps you'd have to take if you wanted to be a successful bank robber and not end up in the slammer.

Based on what we read in the papers, it appears that most bank robberies are not well planned. Most of the robbers seem to get caught. But since we're business people, we're probably smarter than the average bank robber, so we'd plan ours carefully.

First of all, we'd have to choose the right bank. We need one that's a breeze to rob with a lot of cash on hand. It would have to have minimal security with no inside guards. We would want to know where the video cameras are so they could be avoided or made inoperable. We would also want to make it a bank where nobody knows us or would recognize us.

We'd probably want a pretty good disguise. Instead of a ski mask, maybe a wig, sunglasses, and probably the sort of clothing that would just blend in with all of the customers'. We'd want to select the time of day carefully, too—a period when walk-in traffic was at its slowest, like mid-morning when there's less activity would probably be best. We'd want a note to hand to the teller so she wouldn't have to hear your voice ... something that's cleverly written and would get the teller's attention. We'd probably want to choose a weapon in case there's a shoot-out. Maybe a small gun that could be concealed easily and which would scare the teller sufficiently.

We'd probably want a reliable getaway car to get in and out of the bank quickly, and an experienced driver who wouldn't buckle under pressure in case there's a high-speed chase with the local police.

Now, after all this planning, you've got to get up the nerve to go into the bank and pull it off. And once you're inside with your note, your disguise, and your gun, absolutely nothing must go wrong. If you do it right, you've accomplished your goal. You've got instant cash. There could be a lot of it if you did everything correctly. If you did it wrong, there is no second chance. You don't get to try it again—at least not until you're out on parole.

Now, most intelligent people would never seriously consider robbing a bank. Most people don't want to risk doing hard time in jail. It's really a big risk, because most bank robbers are caught sooner or later. Robbing banks is a high profile, high-risk crime with little chance of success and a great chance of getting caught. And if you read the local papers, more and more people seem to be trying it all the time. We see them on television as they are hauled into court; we hear about them being sentenced for attempted robbery and grand theft. They are easily caught because most bank robbers have no plan or forethought and are just plain stupid. They forget about things like traceable bills, hidden alarms, exploding ink packets, or accomplices who would rather turn them in because their payoff wasn't big enough. They leave a trail of clues and mistakes for the police to track. They eventually end up as the losers.

It's amazing how many businesses are a little similar. They moan and complain that business stinks, the economy is bad, sales aren't being made, and money is tight. And each day they complain a little more. It's the government, the high taxes, the unemployment, the elected public officials, and the competition. They have no business plan; they have no marketing plan; they have no sales plan. Each day they open their stores or offices and hope for the best.

Salespeople go out with hopes of cranking some orders, without a goal, a plan, or an alternate plan in case the first one doesn't work. Some store owners open up just hoping for enough walk-in traffic to make it a profitable day. If nobody comes in, it's because of the economy.

We can learn a lot from bank robbers. Successful planning is everything. The only difference is that bank robbers only get one shot. There is no second chance. But in business, if the first plan fails, we get to try another one. We can keep doing it until we get it right. But bank robbers are driven. They're motivated by large amounts of money. And being driven is a definite asset in business. You can do incredible things if you have the right attitude and the right plan. Some of the largest unsolved crimes in history were the result of detailed planning and precise execution. To be driven financially is good, but drive should not be equated with stupidity.

Now the bottom line to this whole thing is: Do you have a marketing plan? Do you know where your new business is coming from? Do you know where your next sale is coming from, and the one after that? Do you have a second plan in case the first one doesn't work?

It's amazing how many businesses will do a promotion without any type of plan at all. It's like shooting from the hip. Business slows down, and right away the "ready, fire, aim" promotions start to come out of the woodwork. No thought, no budget, no plan.

There's one great advantage to planning a promotion properly. We can figure out what doesn't work the first time and correct it to make it better. Proper planning can reduce the risk factor in planning a promotion or just day-to-day business. The next time business slows down, sales get soft, or money isn't coming in, ask yourself: Do we have a plan to make it better? Do we have a step-by-step approach for what to do when the cash isn't coming in as fast as we'd like? Or are we taking the "let's just sit back until things get better" approach to selling?

An increase in the bottom line takes the right plan, the right attitude, hard work, and a lot of luck. And the harder you work at your plan, the luckier you get.

Banging the Drum Can Make Your Cash Register Ring

Here's the scenario. You're at your music store. It's 11:00 a.m. on a Tuesday. There's nobody coming in. You could hear a guitar pick drop. It's so quiet, you can hear the tuning pins in the pianos sigh under the strain of the strings. There are no customers. There is no traffic in the mall. There are no people on the street. The cash register is aching to ring, and the invoices, contract pads, and Visa machines are on idle, just waiting to get into gear. In three more days there will be payroll to meet, taxes to pay, and floor plan to be dealt with. What can we do? What can the salespeople do to be a little more self-productive during the slack periods, to crank a little more business later on in the day, if not right then?

How about this? Let's pull the names of three people who are previous customers we haven't seen for awhile, three people who were just in the store but didn't buy anything, three people who made local news in the morning paper, and three people at random right out of the phone book. That's 12 people total.

Now, let's call the three people we haven't seen for awhile and ask them how they're doing. Then tell them that we've got a new instrument that just arrived, and we'd like to invite them in to see it just to get their opinion about it before we start showing it to the general public. (People love to give opinions, and it's easier than asking them to spend money.)

Then let's call the three people who didn't buy anything last time, and try to get them back one more time. Offer them a freebie. Tell them about something they may have missed. Figure out what will get them back once more that week.

Then drop a note to the three people who made the news that morning, congratulating them on the press they received, and include a discount coupon or offer something of value just for stopping by to see you that week.

Then call the three people right out of the phone book and tell them you need their help. You're new in this business and wonder if they know someone you can send a brochure to who might be interested in a musical instrument. For their help, you'd like to send them a lottery ticket, or something else of interest or of value.

That's nine calls and three notes total. Twelve contacts that won't take very long. Multiply that by five days a week, and you have 60 customer contacts per week. If two or three people did that in your organization on a regular basis, you'd have more than 700 new customer contacts EACH MONTH! If just a small percentage of those people showed up at your store, you'd never be lacking for people walking through your door.

Now what about the slower months of the year? The months are different for each segment of the music industry. Do you have any plans to go outside of your store for business during the year? Home shows, fairs, perimeter sales, mall kiosk promotions? These promotions don't normally require huge budgets, and they sure beat hanging around hoping someone comes in.

If you're going to keep your music store cranking every hour of every day, you've got to have a monthly plan that involves your existing customer base, promoting the accessory side of the music business, an up-to-date teaching program, a lead-generation program, a concert and clinic program, and a PR program.

There are hundreds of ideas for doing more business during the course of a day at your music store. Of course, you have to want to do it. If you're busy all day long, you might have to take a shorter lunch break or give up working the daily crossword puzzle. But you could be taking more money to the bank as a result.

Going Outside of the Store for Extra Sales

I love home shows, especially during cold weather months when there isn't a whole lot else going on. It's a great afternoon of entertainment. Actually, I've never bought a whole lot at home shows. The usual routine is to get a shopping bag or two, fill them up with about 15 pounds of brochures and literature, add 20 or 30 business cards, talk to anybody who wants to make conversation, and forget about them entirely after you get back home. Great fun. Makes for a heck of a day.

Think about the last home show you went to. Did you buy anything? Did anybody even ask you to? How did you feel when you went by a display and the guy was sitting down eating his lunch? Were two or three sales-people talking to each other as if it were a social event? How about the displays where there weren't any salespeople at all? How about the ones that looked like they survived *Animal House*, with dirty, dusty signs, over-flowing ashtrays, and every item, model, and style that the store sells?

My neighbor had a deck built after he went to a local home show. He made a great point when I asked him if he put the deal together at the show. He said, "No, the home show certainly told me who not to deal with." He said that he left his name at one display with a salesperson that never got back to him. Another deck builder was way too expensive. And another wouldn't give him the time of day—all he said was: "When you're really interested, give me a call."

Then there are the consumer events like fairs, home shows, mall shows, and the retail shows where you might find pianos, organs, digital key-boards, karaoke machines, guitars, amps, and all the accessory items. It's nice to look at the instruments and fun to listen to salespeople demonstrating them. Sometimes there are several dealers at one show. Some try to get people to stop. Others are happy when you don't try to intrude on their day.

If you've ever displayed at an outside event, think about how you've done. Are you in category A: "What can we do to talk to a lot of people?" or category B: "How long before we can get the heck out of here?" Be honest.

Standing on your feet for 12 straight hours can be a little bit of a strain, particularly when you're not selling anything. But when you're putting together a lot of sales, getting appointments with people to meet you at the store, accumulating leads, and creating some great visibility in your marketplace, time can go by very quickly.

Some music dealers do a lot of business at home shows, mall shows, and other consumer events. And some would be happy if they never went to another outside exposure ... ever. If you've got the right attitude, the right selling skills, and the right display with the right price points, you can probably do a lot of business. Having the right mind-set is the first step. Wanting to do it is very important.

I remember some very clever instrument displays at various shows. One exhibit had all the salespeople wearing badges that simply said: "Go Ahead, Ask Me." The badge didn't give the person's name or the store's name. It was a neat idea that gave them a different look and gave shoppers the impression that they were easy to talk to.

Treasure chest promotions do really well at consumer events. When you need to get the prospect into your store to close a sale that you can't put together at the show, giving him a key taped to the back of your business card can work wonders. Tell him that if his key opens the lock in the treasure chest at your store within the next week, he'll win the prize inside. It could be dinner for four, movie tickets, a CD player, a guitar or other instrument, an accessory item, or something more valuable.

Free drawings at consumer events can build a great mailing list, develop prospects, and get you immediate sales. If you think they're a waste of time, you're just not doing it right. Leaving a few hundred drawing cards on a table with a few pencils and a handmade sign probably won't generate a lot of interest. But an attended drawing table with professionally painted signs and an appealing giveaway, plus a drawing card that qualifies the person entering the contest, can really get things moving for you. It also helps if you talk to every person who registers.

If home shows, mall shows, and outside consumer events are a pain for you, do yourself and your company a favor: stay home. If you really want to do some business and run circles around your competition at the same time, start planning your next show now. It could really generate some immediate business and give you enough leads to keep prospects coming through your door every day.

Selling Musical Instruments with a Little Class

Last Saturday, I went to the symphony. Now, to you it may not be any big deal, but in all of my years in the music business, I have never gone to the symphony. Classical music is not my bag. It's not that I have anything against symphonic music, it's just that my head is wired for country, and it's my first choice in music ... as well as my second and third.

One of my golfing buddies invited me to join him and his wife. It was not easy to turn down. They have season tickets, and they never asked if it was my type of thing. I think they just assumed that since I had spent 15 years in the music business, I must like that type of music. So I went. I learned a long time ago that sometimes you don't openly admit that country music is your life. Sometimes people spit at you. It's not easy.

For the very few of you who have never been to the symphony, and for the people who share my musical tastes, let me tell you about my evening.

First of all, you dress differently going to the symphony. It's not at all like going to Jim's Place to hear the Gatlin Brothers. No boots. No jeans. No sweatshirts with funny sayings. It's suit, tie, and cuff links. It's soft conversation instead of loud jokes. It's Cabernet Sauvignon instead of Miller Lite.

I went with a completely open mind and was looking forward to expanding my musical horizons. It was a real experience.

The program started at 8:30, and we arrived in our seats at 8:15. The orchestra was already on stage. There were about 90 musicians all decked out in black and white and already playing. It seemed like everyone was playing a different tune. Some were playing fast, some were playing slow, and some were talking to each other as they were playing. Then I found out that this wasn't part of the concert. This was called "warming up." I guess they do this in front of the audience so you know you're getting the number of musicians you paid for.

I glanced through the program that listed the tunes that were going to be played during the show, plus the names of the performers and their respective instruments. Nowhere did I see names like Reba, Willie, Waylon, Ferlin, or Conway. Instead there were names like Kazuyoshi, Ruxandra, Tamara, Marywynn, and Walden.

The list of songs that evening had nothing to do with cheating, dying, pickup trucks, prison, or trains. Instead there were overtures, odes, and themes.

Anyway, at 8:30 on the dot, the side door opened and this fellow with a fiddle came in and walked toward the empty chair to the left of the podium. Obviously he has a lot of clout, because everyone immediately hushed, including the audience. Then, from the back somebody started to play, he started to play, everybody started to play, and in five seconds, they quit. You see, in this type of music, everybody has to be perfectly in tune. "Close enough" is for country ... and rock 'n' roll.

Then, after that hush, the door opened again, and the conductor walked out. Wow. Big applause. Big time. He's in complete control and everybody knows it.

Now, I know at this point you think I'm going to get negative on the music played. But I can't. It was great. Even the guy who sang like his shorts were too tight was good. There was a gal who sang in a pitch that only big dogs could hear, but it was right on. The orchestra was well-rehearsed, everyone knew their instruments to perfection, and each selection was outstanding.

And you know what I liked best about the whole concert? The enthusiasm of the people in the audience. They sincerely liked it. Really! I mean, it was not like a Dwight Yokum concert, where everybody screams and clutches at him and his band when he comes on stage, but it was sincere appreciation for music in its highest form. They loved it. And I shared the same feeling. It was contagious. Everyone was on a high.

I looked at the people in the audience and saw admiration and satisfaction on their faces. No one had to drag them to the hall. There were 3,000 people who loved every minute of it.

Now here's what I think. Those people in the audience ... the people who attend symphony concerts, probably are not in the market to purchase an instrument for themselves, particularly string, brass, or woodwind. But they have a big say in who does and where they go. They have a tremendous amount of leverage when it comes to urging their children or grandchildren to get involved in the school band or orchestra, or to take music lessons.

Why not try to get these people into your music store in any way possible, just to find out who they know or who they can refer? Then try to get those referrals in your store based on that highly respected recommendation of their grandparents or relatives, and you might have more business than you can handle.

But they have to know that you exist first. Then you establish a need, and fill it.

Nowhere in the program for the concert was there a direct response ad for a music store. There was an ad to get a free egg roll after the concert with a same-day symphony ticket, and there were a couple of other coupons and freebies just for coming in the advertiser's store with the program. There were a couple of music stores with an ad saying they were great and that they were nice people, too. But a little more active involvement on a direct marketing basis from music stores might not hurt.

Now before you get too bent out of shape and say, "I donate to the local musical organizations," or "I run an institutional ad in every symphony program," you might think about getting a bigger bang for your buck. How about asking people to come into your store for a particular reason? The restaurants do. The print shops do. Even the symphony itself asks you to come up with bucks.

And you've heard it before ... "if you don't ask, you don't get." My thinking is that you might ask the people who are the most interested ... the ones genuinely interested in music. And if they aren't potential customers, ask who they know, and who they can refer.

Keep those people on your mailing list. Send them a card at Christmas. Invite them to your store regularly. *Try to sell them something.* That's what business is all about.

If you did that on a regular basis, you probably wouldn't have to worry too much about your competition, and you might never again have to run an ad that says ... "Special this week—40% off."

What do you think?

Achieving Your Goals

Occasionally, I ask people what they thought the function of their business was. It was sort of a trick question. I get several different responses, all having to do with turning a profit or making money. I don't think that's what the function of your business should be. The function of your music business should be to create and maintain customers. Your GOAL should be to make a profit. When we start to confuse the function with the goal, things can slip. Everyone in business has different goals. The function should be one of the ways to achieve a goal.

Obviously, goals in business are important when it includes the bottom line. It doesn't matter if it's to increase sales, lower costs, open other stores, or get higher margins. Maybe it's to take on different lines, increase your lesson programs, or develop a more sophisticated Internet presence. Whatever your specific goals are, they aren't going to happen unless you make them happen. This isn't the Lottery where all it takes is a dollar and a dream. This is real life. No dreaming allowed. If you want to achieve your goals, maybe you should start by writing them down, then come up with a plan. You have to be willing to take risks. Uh-oh … risks.

Nobody in the music business wants to have to take a risk unless absolutely necessary. After things don't change, then we think back to what we could have done. I remember the line from the Walter Matthau/Jack Lemmon movie *Grumpy Old Men*. Chuck, the owner of the restaurant where they went ice fishing said, "Never let the only regrets in life be the risks you didn't take." Achieving goals may require taking a risk or two. Maybe more. It also involves taking advantage of opportunity when it presents itself.

I like to stay in touch with music retailers all over the country, just to get a feel for how business is at the immediate moment. Over the past few weeks, these are some of the comments I've heard from various retailers:

"I should have picked a better location for my store."
"I could have had a better month, but my competition was giving the stuff away."
"I would have made my numbers last month, if it wasn't for the construction in front of my store."
"I should have hired a better manager; things would have been different."
"Shoulda, woulda, coulda." Those words become goal killers. They turn goal setters into dreamers. Remember Marlon Brando as Terry Malloy in *On the Waterfront*? "I coulda been a contender. I coulda had class and been somebody."

OK, let me ask you a couple of questions. Does your desire match your goals? Are you willing to take risks? Are you willing to give up something to meet your goals? Maybe it will take longer hours, harder work, or a change in personnel. Also, your level of desire will determine how long it will take to achieve your goals, particularly if it involves money.

In the music business many people are more "needy" than "greedy." Need can be a stronger motivator for achieving goals than desire or want, particularly if you've got a note due at the bank, or the sales tax people want you to sit down and chat.

So, here are some ideas for achieving whatever your goals may be:

1) Whatever your goal is, write it down. Any time an idea pops into your head, write it down. If you see it on paper it will make more sense, become more realistic and easier to achieve.

2) Make sure you have the intention to go after it. Intentions precede actions. If you don't intend to go after your goal, why bother to have it to begin with? Desire is a tremendous factor in achieving your goals

3) You need persistence and the patience to achieve what you want. Not giving up falls in here somewhere. Sometimes it means shifting gears, changing your plan of action, or coming up with a different set of ideas.

4) If you want something bad enough, you will always find a way to get it. I don't care what it is. Maybe it's to own your own jet, learn a second language, be the mayor of your town, or retire at an early age. No matter how far-fetched any goal may be, it's attainable if you want it bad enough. And that might require giving up something … maybe a lot of something.

5) Here's the kicker for achieving goals—passion. You have to really love what you do, and that's where people in the music business have the edge. We love what we do. It's fun. It's exciting. There's nothing like being in our business.

So, let's write down a couple of goals right now. See if you really intend to go after them, or are just giving them lip-service. See if you have the persistence and drive to get what you're after. And then ask yourself how bad you want to achieve them. You might be surprised at what the answer is. And if you want whatever your goals are bad enough, you'll get what you're trying to achieve.

"I'm Sorry ... Our Employees Are Stupid"

C'mon now. You wouldn't ever say that to a customer, would you? Would you even infer it? Say it about a fellow worker? Criticize the ineptness of a salesperson? It just doesn't sit well, even if it's true. It makes a customer want to run—and it happens all the time.

I sent some flowers about a week ago to a friend of mine in another city. I asked my local florist to make sure they were delivered from a florist within a few miles of the recipient, and I carefully spelled out the message for the card. The flowers ended up being delivered late, from a town 20 miles away, and the message was misspelled. The person getting the flowers thought it was from someone else. I called the local florist where I had placed my order and the response was, "Some of the people here are so stupid." I should have just found a florist in the other city myself, and handled it over the phone.

I took my car in to have one of the fog light bulbs replaced. I even called in advance to make sure it was in stock. When I stopped in on the way to work, I told them I'd wait. Really, how long could a bulb replacement take? Suddenly I noticed my car being moved out of the garage and onto the back lot. I asked the service manager what was going on, and he said he'd look into it. After about 15 minutes he told me that the bulb was not in stock after all, and it would take about an hour and a half to find one and install it. I asked him why they told me otherwise on the phone, and why didn't they tell me when they realized their error? They knew I was waiting. His reply? "Some of these guys are so dumb." Sure makes me want to refer my friends there.

It's not just this area of the country, even though the northeast has its share of testy people. I called JetBlue airlines to make a reservation. I found out that they don't have a central call center; the calls are directed to individual reservation agents in their homes. They work out of their bedrooms or studies. The reason I know this is because when I called for a reservation, the female agent was yelling, "Get out of this room, now!" She was talking to her kids. I asked her about it, and she replied, "Those kids never listen ... they are so stupid." Makes JetBlue look like Southwest Airlines on a bad day. At least Southwest tries to be funny. This woman's brain was going into "tilt."

I went into CompUSA yesterday to buy a new laptop computer. The floor model I was looking at was priced at $2,199. Although it was locked securely in place by burglar bars, it looked like it had been banged around once or twice, and some of the keys were missing. I asked the salesperson what happened and was told, "You know how customers are … and some of the salespeople are just as bad." I don't know what that meant, and I didn't want to be put in the category of being destructive or … stupid, so I just left.

Do you think these are isolated incidents? If so, maybe that's because you get along with the other people in your business, have respect for them, and treat them like peers. But in many cases, a quick-temper, short fuse, or just being fed up with customers for the moment can let this happen. It's so easy to blame somebody else to save face for yourself. The problem is, that it doesn't save face for your business. The answer is to forget all the rhetoric of placing the blame and do whatever is necessary to make the customer feel better. It could be an apology, a partial refund, or just getting the customer to be your friend and understand it from your side.

I was at Home Depot trying to buy a piece of lighting equipment; it was on display, but appeared to be out of stock. I asked one of the associates to help me. They said it wasn't in stock and to return in a week. He left, and I noticed several boxes way up high. You'd need a tall ladder or forklift to get up there, but there they were. He just didn't want to close down the aisle, get the lift, and get one down. So I mentioned to the manager that I couldn't get the help I needed. The manager said, "I'm sorry, what can I do to make you feel better?" I replied, "Let me have one for half-price, apologize for your clerk's ineptness, have him fired, and check me out without standing in line."

The manager offered, "How about we just have him stand at the end of the aisle and you can throw something at him? I'll give you 10% off too, and get you in a line with our best-looking female cashier. At least you'll have something nice to look at while you wait." Then he yelled, "Jake, come over here, you have a hostile customer!"

I let Jake keep his job, told him I really wasn't a bad guy, took the discount, and told my friends how good the manager was. He never told me his people were stupid. He just let me know he was doing whatever he could to get me to come back. He made me laugh, too.

Sometimes it can be simple to appease a customer—without ridiculing or blaming someone on your staff or in your business. You're part of a professional, well-run business. Isn't that the image you want to project? So the next time you want to spew about someone else's inadequacies in your organization, count to 10 … then, don't say anything at all. Just do what it takes to correct the situation yourself. Everyone will look better for it.

How Well Do You Know Your Products?

One of my TVs developed a problem the other day—it started buzzing and wheezing when it was first turned on. I figured I'd just go out and buy a new one. I didn't know where to go, so I decided to go to a major department/discount/electronics store. I thought, "Hey, everybody discounts these things—and how bad could their prices be?"

I guess it's been a while since I've seen what's currently available: flat screens, high definition television, and pictures that are so realistic that you can practically reach inside the screen and touch them. I was impressed. So many different sets, different sizes, and different brands. Hundreds of sets all tuned to the same channel.

I found a 20-inch TV that had a very sharp picture. The price was more than the other 20-inch models. I needed help; I wanted feature and benefit information. There was nobody around to explain why I should pay the extra bucks—I couldn't even find someone to attempt to get their attention. So, after waiting around with cash in my hand, I went over to one of the registers where they ring up the big stuff. No one was around there, either.

I saw a telephone near the register, so I picked it up and called the store. (How handy, the store number was right on the phone). I explained my predicament, that I wanted to buy a TV but there was no one there to help me. There was no explanation, nor an apology, but the next thing I know, over the PA system comes "There's a customer in TV who needs help." Then click, dial tone. I was very proud of myself. I thought that my solution to getting some customer service should be put in their flyers and brochures. Not too many people are that quick-thinking.

Next thing I know, a younger gentleman (still eating a sandwich) is coming over to me. He said, "Whassup?" (Sort of sounded like something out of a bad beer commercial.) I pointed to the set, and asked him why it was more expensive than the others. He replied, "Flat screen," So I said, "Why does that make it better?" And at that point he pulled a card from underneath the set and began to read it to me. I said, "I can read. Why should I pay more?" And he just kept reading. I figured that if this was the extent of his product knowledge, I really should just shop for price.

I asked him if I could use his phone. He said OK. I called the store's competitor right from the store, gave them the make and model I was looking at, and asked the price. It was cheaper. I hung up, went there, and bought it.

I felt good about it, too. They didn't read to me. They explained the features I had asked about—they actually knew and understood the product. I know I can be a pain-in-the-neck customer. But at that point I felt justified in my purchase decision. The "whassup" salesperson would have been better off in a job where you had to ask, "You want fries with that?"

The problem I see is that this has also happened to me at a major office supply discount store—I asked a question, and they read to me from a card about the product that was in plain sight. Same thing at one of those big-box warehouse stores when I asked about a vacuum cleaner. Pull the tag off the shelf and read it to the customer.

There is a simple solution to this. If your employees don't know your products inside and out, then teach them, train them, or get new employees. Nothing shouts "unprofessional" like a salesperson who reads from a brochure, point-of-sale card, or shelf-talker that a customer can read for themselves. Customers want to know features, benefits, and even the opinion the salesperson might have about the product. They want their desire to be built up so much that price will be secondary. Uh-oh, does that mean everybody doesn't buy on price?

Ask yourself this: If the high-ticket item you want to buy from a well-educated, likeable salesperson is $889, and you can buy the same item across town for $875 from a less-than-knowledgeable salesperson who treats you like you're an intrusion on his or her day, are you really going to make the 15-mile trek to save 14 bucks? I'm sure some people might, but the majority won't if the other salesperson knows their stuff. A salesperson's personality and product knowledge are important to a customer spending serious money. Price could often be secondary.

So if you're thinking, "What if I train my salespeople so they know everything about all the products, and I train them to sell, then they end up leaving?" Then ask yourself this: "What if I don't—and they stay?" Now, there's something to think about.

CHAPTER 3:
The Competition

Outsmarting Your Competition

I saw a report the other evening on CNN about how to outsmart your retail competition, particularly those stores whose main marketing concept is price. The report said that price isn't everything. Other things enter the equation, such as selection and service. It specifically mentioned Wal-Mart, and it said the answer to outsmarting Wal-Mart was "by not trying to."

That advice sounds counterintuitive, but the report said the secret to retailers' survival in a Wal-Mart world isn't about attempting to outrun the 800-pound retail gorilla but about the ability to maneuver around it.

I don't know if your competition is a gorilla, but even if you don't have a Guitar Center or Sam Ash in your backyard, chances are you've got at least a few chimpanzee competitors in your town, not to mention Internet competition making for an unlevel playing field.

The CEO of one successful Wal-Mart competitor quoted in the report described his strategy: "It's like the two outdoorsmen who wake to find a raging bear at their campsite," he said. "One camper slowly stands and backs away; the other starts to lace up his sneakers. 'You can't outrun the bear!' whispers the first. 'I don't have to,' replies the second. 'I just have to outrun you!'"

Competing with Wal-Mart, the world's largest retailer, on price alone is futile. Wal-Mart's mantra of "everyday low prices" may as well be written in stone. That's how it has pounded its rivals and built its $288 billion retail empire, by setting prices not just below the competition but close to rock bottom, while still making a profit. "Wal-Mart clearly wins on price, and to a lesser degree, selection, but nowhere else," the report said. "Price isn't everything."

According to CNN, these retailers have successfully managed to "co-exist and even thrive" in the same forest as Wal-Mart because they focused not just on boosting sales but on becoming the best in terms of quality, product selection, in-store service, and convenient locations.

"Two-thirds of shoppers find Wal-Mart's assortments, middling product quality, and limited services not worth the savings," the report said. "That means, regardless of Wal-Mart's proximity, there are plenty of customers looking for alternatives." After reading this, I thought of many ways to handle the competition without having to give instruments away.

Here's a suggestion: Google the phrase "Competing with Wal-Mart." You will be amazed at the strategies and ideas that come up. Then put some of the ideas to use on a smaller scale with your music store at your local level.

Be what your competitors are not. If you go head-to-head with your competition, it's going to be an uphill battle. Take a good look at the various revenue sources you have, whether it be instruments, print music, lessons, or accessories. What can you do or offer better than anyone else? How can you reach customers in ways your competition doesn't?

The underlying message with small guys fighting with the big box stores is: "Going head-to-head on price alone is a recipe for disaster." You are not going to win.

No matter how big your store is, you cannot carry everything. You can only carry so many accessories. New ones are appearing by the minute. Many big music stores don't carry vintage guitars, acoustic pianos, specialized digital keyboards, accordions, didgeridoos, zithers, alp horns, an extensive print music selection, etc.

How about lessons? Not all music stores give bass trombone lessons, vocal lessons, class lessons, adult-only group lessons, musical kindergarten classes, and so on.

You get the picture. You want to compete in arenas in which other stores aren't playing. You can be a major leaguer in a minor league ballpark by thinking outside the box, and you can make a lot more profit on something few stores carry than you can worrying about selling your next $99 guitar.

Once you find a formula for making good margins and creating decent profit for yourself, don't stop. You continually have to be on your toes to make sure your competition isn't catching up. You want to stay ahead of your competition down the street, while they get eaten up by the we-sell-for-less guys. You've got to constantly tweak your inventory, your programs, and your game plan to stay ahead of what might be coming behind you.

A few nights ago I had the opportunity to hear Dorsey Levens, a former Super Bowl star with the Green Bay Packers, speak at his induction into our local sports hall of fame. He played at a local high school, and he credited his coaches and teammates for his success on and off the field. He said it was a "continual learning experience." His exact words were, "When you stop improving, you're done." When you stop improving your competition has a chance to catch up. In other words, when you're green, you're growing; when you're ripe, you rot.

Next time you think you have to go head-to-head with the music store down the street, across town, or on the Internet … don't. Let everyone else fight it out. Find out what you can do better and different, then let your margins speak for themselves.

"Outclubbing" Your Competition

Competition can be good for your business. It's better though, when you're the competitor who's driving the market, rather than the business that's being outdriven by the guys down the street. You need the right ammunition, and you need the right clubs. "Outclubbing" your competition does not mean beating them to death. It just means using a different approach, a different tactic, a creative way to achieve better results.

Think of it this way: a golfer does not always use a driver off the tee on every par four. It depends on how the hole is set up. Sometimes it's a three or five wood and a longer iron for a better chance of keeping it in the fairway. In tennis, a stronger serve might not be the answer—using an oversized racket might take up where a weaker backhand left off. In business, it's not low prices or a bigger store; it's being where your competition is not. It means doing well where they don't excel. It means sometimes using a different stick or I guess, "shtick."

What is your business's strongest niche? What sets you apart from your competition? What can you do in a different way to dramatically increase your revenue?

The cruise industry continues to grow and more cruise ships are being built each year. Bigger and better ships are coming out with plenty of cabins that are going to have to be filled. In 1998, Carnival Cruise Lines took a big step. They introduced the Paradise—the first totally nonsmoking ship to sail the Caribbean. It holds more than 2,000 passengers. You sign a release form stating that you understand it is a non-smoking ship, smoking is not permitted, and if you are caught with smoking material in your possession, you are fined $250, put off at the next port, and you figure out your own way home. On some cruises as many as a dozen people are escorted off the ship. This ship is booked solid every time it leaves Miami. People love it. Carnival thought outside the box and took a chance that paid off.

The hardware super stores are multiplying like rabbits. Home Depot and Lowes are popping up in cities with as little as 30,000 residents. But some of the smaller hardware guys are not lying down and playing dead. They just reshuffle and do what the big guys can't. Some concentrate on small engine repair, unique and unusual tools, hard-to-find parts, used equipment, and lots of "you-don't-have-to-walk-two-miles-to-find-it" selections. Not to mention that you can park near the front door instead of in the next zip code.

There are automobile dealerships and showrooms that are starting to be the size of football fields. They have coffee shops and amusement areas. They use golf carts to get people out to the acres of cars on the lot. But Car Max and AutoNation didn't scare the pants off of the local guys. The smaller dealers just concentrated on better service. They capitalized on knowing their customers better, and stayed in touch with them more regularly.

They also learned that it isn't always a heavily discounted price that gets the sale. Some customers want personal attention, a free ride to the airport, and the "we know you by your first name" atmosphere.

In the music business, grand pianos are not only highly competitive, but in many cases it's become a huge discount business. There's Armory Sales, College Sales, and all kinds of Liquidation Sales. The public is starting to think that you've got to be crazy to pay list for a grand piano. Cooper Music of Atlanta brings another club out of the bag by offering to hold a concert in your own home with the purchase of a grand, and you can invite as many people as you want. Many of these people could be future prospects. And they can be sold on something other than price.

Fletcher Music Centers of Florida sell electronic home organs the way Arthur Murray dance studios sell dance lessons. It's free group lessons with a party atmosphere. They create their own customers and their own market, in a business that practically doesn't exist anymore.

For the smaller guitar stores that can't compete with large chains, vintage guitars could be the answer. It's selling a selected audience high-ticket, high-profit instruments on a one-to-one basis. Music-Go-Round proved used instruments can set them apart from other music stores.

When new competition rolls into town or your current competition tries to go after your customers, competing on price alone doesn't always work. It might be time to start thinking about sneaking up on them instead of hitting them head-on. Try a few different tactics. The "outclub" instead of "out-discount" approach could work.

Going Where Your Competition Is Not

I had a very interesting conversation a few weeks ago with Don Middleton, owner of Don's Musicland in Peoria, Illinois. I had seen his website which included some information about his store. In the "Info About Us" section, reads:

"Elvis Presley, Johnny Cash, Chet Atkins, and The Beatles all played in Peoria right through the fingertips of Don Middleton. If you were a guitarist here in the mid-1970s, you already knew this because Don taught you how to play the songs that these guys wrote. During the day, he drove a towel truck, but at night, his hands rested on the maple neck and rosewood fretboard of a Gibson 335 ES, and his heart drove to the beat of Roy Clark.

"In 1968, Don bought Hill's Music from Billy Hill with one simple goal: never go broke. Four locations and 35 years later, he looks back and wonders how it all came together. 'It was different back then. I didn't really have any money, but Billy was a good guy, and we worked something out. The only condition was that I had to move the store,' says Don.

"That original location, 3516 California Street, is now part of the downstate medical center, and Don's new store, the biggest to date, is open for business on North University. For the most part, however, his clientele has remained the same. In the '70s, everyone wanted to be a rock star. Now those guys all have families, and they keep coming in to rebuy their old instruments. Even people who have moved to Chicago bring their guitars back for us to take a look at them."

After reading this on the website, I thought to myself that this guy has a real handle on the guitar business today, so I wanted to talk with him. I called, and Don himself answered the phone. (I was surprised to get a human being right off the bat.) I asked Don his thoughts on the music industry today, and he said that price is the biggest factor today. The mentality is "how cheap can you make it, how cheap can you sell it?" Imports have knocked the profit right out of the guitar business.

Now here's what floored me about our conversation. Don told me that two years ago he took on Lowrey organs. He sells them to the mature market. His actual statement was, "For what I make on one mid-level Lowery organ, I would have to sell 93 guitars." I tried to tell him that the organ business doesn't exist today, but he wouldn't listen. He said he had a lady in her 70s search him out on the Internet, just to find out where his store was. She had a 25-year old Kimball she wanted to trade in. She came to his store and bought a new Lowrey. Jeesh! Who would have thought? I asked Don what his second line of organs was. He said "used." There aren't too many manufacturers of home organs around anymore.

Actually outside of Lowrey, Roland, and Hammond, I guess he's right. But to be successful and make a lot of money in a business that more-or-less doesn't exist, Don says that you need a program to bring people into the store and keep them playing. You need a system that works. Lowrey and Roland do this. Don says "The same people/customers are out there, just like in the organ golden years. You just have to find them." He says, "It's amazing how many of the organ dealers who are still out there today are very profitable. He told me that the few organ dealers out there today talk to each other and try to help each other. No discount ads. No cut-throat Internet competition. Just get them in, teach them to play, and step them up.

Think about this: What are you doing today that sets your music store apart from the competition? Do you have something different where you can compete in a different arena and control the margins? But, hang on. Being different means finding your own niche. It doesn't have to be the home organ business. No music store can stock everything. What niche market can you fill? Vintage guitars? Unique percussion instruments? Cajun accordions? High-quality brass and reed instruments? Where can you excel? The finest teaching staff? The most complete accessory department in the area? The biggest musical gift department in the state? A comprehensive selection of sheet music? Do you have dedicated personnel to service that area of your store?

I'm not saying you have to give up the $100 guitars, but man, you got to sell a lot of them just to make payroll. The electronics thing is worse. Your competition is nationwide with dealers who will ship anywhere (without having to charge sales tax). Wouldn't it be nice to make 60-70 points on something there is little competition for, on a regular basis?

Finding a specialty niche is one of the many ideas that would work for getting more margin per sale, but there are a lot of other ideas for bringing more people through your door as well. (Particularly ideas that don't cost much to implement). I think there are new ideas for creating more customers coming up every day, especially customers your competition doesn't know exist.

The Mass Market Stores Are in a Different World

If you look through the back issues of *Music Trades*, there has been a lot of concern about stores such as Wal-Mart, Costco, Target, and Sam's Club getting into the musical instrument business. The fear is that they will sell instruments at giveaway prices and steal customers right out from under our noses.

Really? Are they that much better at marketing? Do they do that great of a job, sell stuff cheap, and run rings around the little guys? At the risk of sounding too much like Andy Rooney, let me tell you what I found when I went shopping at some of the big chain stores during the past couple of weeks.

First stop was Macy's. Macy's is all over the country now, instead of at just one flagship store on 34th Street in Manhattan. Recently they took over the Kaufman's department stores in Syracuse, New York's local malls. I went in looking for a Cuisinart appliance advertised in their Sunday newspaper insert. I liked the product, liked the price, and just wanted to buy it.

I couldn't find it. There was no one in the housewares department, so I went to the "customer service/register" desk to ask. There was a lady ahead of me with the same circular being told that everything in the ad wasn't available, so that kind of set the tone for what I was going to hear. Nancy, who was obviously overburdened, asked if she could help me. Nancy told me she had never seen the product, never sold one, and knew nothing about it. That's it … kind of "too bad for you." I asked, "Do other stores have one?" She said, "Beats me." I said, "Can you call and check?" She said (and get this), "I can call all right, but they never pick up their phone in that department."

Nancy did call another store, hit the extension, and she was right … no one answered. I said, "This sure wasn't like this when it was Kaufman's. Now it's more like Target." She answered, "It's like Target, only with higher prices." (No kidding; I'm not making this up.) I ended up buying the product from a smaller retailer, who even explained how to use the appliance for me. So much for Macy's.

Next stop was BJ's Wholesale Club. They're kind of like Sam's Club or Costco. I wanted a 32-inch Aiwa TV with built-in DVD player that was advertised in their mailer. Of course, there was no sales help down the TV aisle, but there was a customer telling people he had just bought one and brought it back because it didn't work. No salesperson bothered to cork this guy up, because everyone was busy elsewhere. Or maybe they were on a break.

I decided I would go someplace where I could get more information on what I was buying, but, since I was there, I noticed in the BJ's mailer a Yamaha DGX520B 88-note keyboard with semi-weighted keys and stand for $599. I wanted to see it, so I went to their musical instrument/office supply aisle. Yep, there it was. It was positioned at eye-level so you could touch the keys and hear the sounds. Actually a lot of people had previously touched the keys, because they were very dirty. One of the buttons was broken off. I did find a clerk/associate to ask about features. This gentleman (whose last job might have been a convenience store) said, "I don't know nuttin' about them things. I wouldn't know what to do wid it if I had it." There were also a few "ya knows" thrown in—you get the idea.

There is a lot to be said for smaller retailers. You just have to let people know you exist and what benefits you provide if you want to compete in today's market. Ralph Waldo Emerson said, "If a man can write a better book, preach a better sermon, or make a better mousetrap than his neighbor, though he builds his house in the woods, the world will make a beaten path to his door." We usually just hear about the mousetrap part, which is probably the most relevant to music retailers.

In any case, Emerson was wrong.

With the media and information overload of the 21st century, you can't just have a better or cheaper product and expect the world to discover you. If you're going to compete with the big guys, you have to get the word out about why you're better. You need to market, promote, and network. You have to use the Internet and e-mail to your best advantage.

While the mass merchants are blowing their brains out with mailers and flyers, you can do the same without draining your ad budget by concentrating on one customer at a time and letting him or her do some of the work for you. A happy, satisfied customer will tell six more people. An unhappy, dissatisfied customer will tell 20. Selling a musical instrument today takes more than just a low price.

Competing with mass merchants takes teaching, explaining, and servicing after the sale. It also takes getting people to like you. Very often when people like you and consider you a friend, price will be secondary. Even if mass merchants start skimming the market, there still will be plenty left over. We just have to go after it. We have to work to beat our own path to our door so customers can find us.

CHAPTER 4:
Customer Service

Bigger Isn't Better, Better Is Better

A Best Buy store just opened in our town. Sears, Home Depot, and quite a few of the other "big box" stores have already been around here for awhile. Every time a new one comes riding into town, the smaller retailers get nervous. Some of the smaller guys end up closing. But some of the independents make the big guys nervous instead. We've seen big name stores fail, too. Bigger is not better. Only better is better. Bigger locations do not always mean better service. You can't always have a close relationship with your customers if you're only working on price and volume.

Online shopping has become the hip thing to do. It's another kind of big-box store with low prices, two-day delivery, and no sales tax in some cases. Everything seems fine and dandy until the complaints start up. Wrong item. Couldn't return it easily. Couldn't get a human being on the line for

information. More than just a small percentage of people were unhappy. Twenty percent or more tried to make returns. Sometimes personal one-on-one can have an advantage.

One of the major mistakes the super stores make is in inventory control. Check it out for yourself. If you're a little guy competing with the Goliaths, here's where you can shine.

Over the weekend, I went shopping for a clock radio with big numbers so I don't have to put my glasses on to see the clock when I wake up. I also wanted to buy an easy-to-use cordless phone for an elderly relative. So I went to Best Buy. Even though there were a lot of clock radios on display, very few boxes were underneath. Thirty percent of the clocks on display were not in stock. But the display models were still there.

So, I went over to the cordless phone department. Instantly I saw one that would be perfect. On the receiver was a tag that read: "This is not a working model. Display only." No working models in boxes were anywhere to be found. I tried to get someone's attention to ask about this, but all the blue polo shirts running around the store seemed to have their own agendas: Look busy. Avoid all eye contact. Whatever you do, don't talk to customers. I saw one clerk coming down the aisle wearing his "Best Buy" name tag. As he walked by without looking at me, I stepped out right in front of him. It was great. I almost knocked him down. Dennis Rodman would have been proud. I sure got his attention. I found out that he was the department manager.

When I asked him how I could buy the phone I was interested in, it was like I had asked him to take a pay cut. He mumbled under his breath, grabbed an inventory control number, went to a computer, and five minutes later, told me there were four on order. He didn't know when they'd be in. I asked him, "Why is it on display if there are none in stock?" He said he could give me four or five reasons: stock was lean, trucks weren't coming in, snow was on the roads, and it was two months after the holidays. I left a few other things I had intended to buy on the floor and walked out.

I went to Sears. Another phone on display. No inventory in stock. I asked if I could buy the display model. The clerk said, "No." I told him I was stealing it, but would leave the money at the register. He had no sense of humor. The salesperson would have probably gotten really nasty if he hadn't been busy watching a ball game on TV. I was sorry to have interrupted him.

I ended up buying both the phone and the clock radio at a small independent retailer who has been in town for 30 years. His prices were competitive. He didn't have any inventory on display that he could not sell. He told me he heard those complaints about the competition all the time, and when something is out of stock in his store, it's off the shelf. Employee turnover is rampant at the chain stores, but his people have been around for years. They get to know the customers, help them with their purchases, and give them the information they need. Guess what? Customers who walk into this store almost always buy. He feels his little store has staying power. Eleven "giants" have come and gone since he's been open.

There are several morals to the story here. If you are a big box store, don't tick off the customer. Don't have something on display that the customer can't buy. Try to help the customer. If you're a small retailer, nothing will beat a close relationship, real service, and a "going out of your way" attitude to help the customer. There's a lot of business out there. Your customers will end up deciding which businesses stay, and which ones will ride out into the sunset. They decide by buying or walking out.

Help! That Crying Child Is Ruining My Sale

Nothing can destroy a sale more than an out-of-control child who starts to act up while a sales presentation is being made. We've all been there. The parents come in with their kids in tow, looking to spend some serious money, when all of a sudden a toddler decides enough is enough. They're no longer in your demo, your presentation, your instruments, or you. Their nerves are plucked, their attention span is way past over, and you find that a three-year-old is starting to take control of the sale. You want to put a deal together—they want out. Or maybe the problem is not a temper-tantrum toddler, but a kid who feels that they have free run of the store. Those displays are their playground. They're running, jumping, kicking, rolling, and sometimes destroying anything they can touch. And through all of this we have to maintain our composure and try to get the customer to buy—all while keeping an eye on the little terror. It's not easy.

I asked several top salespeople on how they handle this type of situation. It is not surprising that the best answers and suggestions came from people who are parents themselves. They are not just good at this; some of them are terrific. And most of them learned these techniques from experiences with their own children. I was surprised to find out that some were totally ready for any-thing that came their way with less-than-tolerable tykes. Here are 10 of the better ideas. Pick the ones you like the best:

- Acknowledge them—Make eye contact with the child or children. Let them feel they're part of the family, the presentation, and the moment.

- Smile—Kids know when you're a grouch. Maybe you're not a big meanie, but little kids don't know that until they figure it out for themselves.

- Drawing supplies—Keep some crayons, coloring books, and plain sheets of paper ready for them to color or draw. Even a magic marker with a plain sheet of white paper can keep a child entertained for a long time.

- Blocks, Legos, dolls—Have a couple of toys in your desk drawer that small kids might like to play with. It doesn't have to be anything fancy. A puzzle with large pieces could be just as effective as the Nintendo Wii.

- Cookies, crackers—Buy a few boxes of animal crackers and keep them in a drawer. Nothing stops a screaming kid faster than finding something else to put in his mouth. Makes sure you get the parents' permission before handing them any type of food.

- Cartoons—A 12-inch TV set with built-in VCR, along with a few Disney videos, could give you an hour of uninterrupted sales dialogue. Have a few child-sized chairs facing a TV in one corner of your store. Make sure the TV is placed so the kids only see the TV, not anything else that's going on. Then just set them and forget them.

- Paper towels, tissues, napkins, handy wipes—If parents come in with tiny tykes, these items will be invaluable. The idea, though, is not to have to scramble to find them. In case of an accident, make it seem like this happens every day. It's no problem. Here's a tissue, now let's get back to the sales presentation.

- Comics, Disney books, Golden books, picture books—Kids like to read, or at least look at the pictures. This might not hold their attention for as long as a movie, but you could get at least 10 minutes of uninterrupted talk time if you have something that grabs their interest.

- Something kids can take home—Obviously you don't want them carting out the TV set, or your best children's books, but any little gift you can give children to take with them will make them, as well as their parents, feel special.

- Bathroom facilities—As soon as the parents come in with the kids, let them know that you have a restroom "just in case." Address the situation before it poses a problem. Wet pants will totally ruin a major sale.

Not everybody can deal with screaming, crying, spoiled, little sale-killing kids—whose parents think they're angels, of course. Sometimes you just want to yell, "Don't you know your kids are brats?" Or maybe the children really are under control, but are just bored out of their mind. Just keep your composure. Stay sane. Not all salespeople can handle difficult children during a sales presentation. But those who can are so good at it that sometimes they sell rings around everyone else in the store. Check out your child-friendly demeanor, atmosphere, and selling area. Bet you can find one or two ways to make it easier to sell to parents who are juggling toddlers at their side.

Attitude Really Makes the Difference

A new McDonald's just opened up not too far from where I live. It's not the ordinary, everyday McDonald's, but more of a theme park, virtual reality, "Ronald McDonald-on-steroids" wonder center. They've been advertising on radio, television, and in all the local print media. They're giving away all kinds of prizes, like trips to Paris, movie passes, home entertainment equipment, and a Rolls Royce. Well, not a real Rolls. I just made that up. But with all the hype, it sure seems like everything is on a "larger-than-life" scale.

I stopped there for lunch the other day. There was a ton of people. There were so many people that I had a hard time finding where the lines to the cash registers really were. Finally, I got to the counter where a young woman who looked liked she may have just signed up for her driver's permit asked if she could help me. As I ordered, another young person that was screaming orders and instructions from the kitchen area repeatedly distracted her. At the same time, another teenager with a Madonna-type headset came running by screaming, "Where the hell are the fries? I need fries!" Someone else turned and yelled, "Get your own damn fries! I just had to box my own apple pies."

It wasn't pleasant. I ordered a salad, and my server said, "We don't have any made-up salads left. It will take a while. Want anything else?"

I didn't want to ruin her whole day, so I ordered something else, along with an apple pie.

She said, "They're two for a dollar."

I said, "I only want one."

She groaned and said, "OK, I'll try to work it out."

I could see that dividing by two was a real problem for her.

In the midst of more screaming and yelling from the back, and a little hissing, snarling, and screeching at the front counter, my order came up. But it had two apple pies. Foolishly, I called it to the attention of Miss Out-of-Control, who said, "Well, what do you want me to do about it? They're two for a dollar."

Not wanting to make her day any worse than it obviously was already, I picked up one of the boxes and said, "Let's see; it says on your name tag that your name is Jessica?"

She replied, "Yeah … ?"

So I took out a pen and wrote on the box: "To Jessica, from Bob." And since it was the holiday season, I wrote: "Happy Holidays!" And since I was on a roll, I drew a smiley face.

She looked at me and said, "Think you're cute, don't you?"

Well, the answer is "yes." I think I can be cute, funny, easygoing, semi-charming, and a little on the less-than-serious side. When I'm the customer, I guess I can be whatever I want to be at the time. McDonald's had gotten me into their mega-burger play palace the first time, but I'm not going back; at least not for a long time, not until Jessica finds a job that is less demanding and where "works well with others" is not part of the criteria for advancement.

Now don't get me wrong. The food was OK. It was typical McDonald's fare. The price was … heck, I don't even know what the price was. I don't know how much McDonald's charges for a Coke, or a shake, or fries, or a Big Mac. I don't care. I order, give them money, and sometimes I get change. Price is not an issue. I had to get two of something, even though I wanted one. Big deal. It's not the end of the world. But attitude is what brings people back.

You can have the lowest prices, the biggest inventory and the most grandiose advertising. You can have slick direct mail, an easy-to-get-to location and a state-of-the-art facility. You'll get people in, and maybe even sell them the first time. But customers would rather go to the dentist for a root canal than go back to a salesperson with a rotten attitude. Customers go back to salespeople they like, who treat them well, and who have smiles on their faces, and good attitudes about their jobs. Customers don't like to face people who wish they worked someplace else, are having a bad day, or can't wait until it's time to go home.

In the music business, customers come in to make a major purchase. Money can be an issue, but more often than not, it is not the main issue. People buy from salespeople they can trust. They buy from salespeople who know their products inside and out. And they buy from salespeople who really love the business they're in. They go out of their way to avoid salespeople who complain about their jobs, dislike their stores, hate their employers, or have the weight of the world on their shoulders. And they hate to deal with salespeople who are continually having a bad day.

Do a quick attitude check. What's your "smile frequency"? Do you really like your job? When you wake up in the morning, are you really anxious to get to the store, or would you rather be selling a different product, or maybe not be in sales at all? When customers tell you they can buy a similar instrument cheaper down the street, how do you react? Do you start to simmer inside? And when you lose a sale to a competitor, do you take it out on the next customer who's looking for a lower price? Do you carry any personal problems from home into your office?

When business slows down, when your competition is giving the stuff away, when customers start asking for lines you don't carry, when nasty customers start making you their entertainment for the day, how do you react? Do you lash back, sneer, and snarl and wish you were doing something else? Or do you hang in there with a good attitude, knowing things will get better?

Abraham Lincoln once said, "It's not what happens to you, it's how you handle what happens to you that determines your happiness in life." Life's too short to have to deal with a bad attitude—particularly when it's yours. A good attitude will help bring customers back one more time. With a bad attitude, you may never see them again.

You Don't Know Jack

Something interesting is going on. Consumers seem to be rebelling against too much technology. Cell phone sales are off. Gateway computers are on a slide. Dot-coms are not getting the anticipated hits. It takes three weeks to learn how to use a palm device that replaces a calendar and address book—only to see it outdated two weeks later because something smaller, faster, and cheaper has been invented.

Customers can take only so much techno info before their brains start to overload. There are computers, refrigerators, microwaves, digital keyboards, digital cameras, digital answering machines, stereos, DVDs, and VCRs—not to mention the owner's manuals that look like pages from a bar exam. It seems that *nothing* is simple anymore. There was a cartoon from *The Far Side* where a student in class was raising his hand frantically, and asked the teacher if he could be excused because his "brain was full." It's not just how much technical data we have stored in our brains that's starting to be a problem; it's how much time we spend studying, reading, watching, listening, and learning about new technology that takes hours out of our day, years out of our lives, and drains our wallets.

I truly believe that the simpler you make it for the customer to understand your product, the easier it is to sell. The problem many times is that the salesperson knows so much about their product (sometimes taking months to figure out), that they expect to cram it into the brain of the customer in three minutes or less. And it doesn't work that way. Customers are starting to go for easier and simpler, rather than complicated—and that's where my friend Jack comes to mind.

Jack is a little-above-middle-aged male, with a few bucks in his pocket. He tends to be a little selective when spending those bucks, but the fact of the matter is, he *does* spend them. He has lots of toys and lots of nice things. But Jack will not buy a product he cannot fully understand while it is being explained to him in a store. He doesn't like to waste time reading directions. He's never read the owner's manual to his car. He can't (or doesn't want to) program his VCR. He will not do business with a company that has an automated answering system where you can't press 0 and get a live person. He will not buy a product from a salesperson who talks in techno-babble, or from anyone who treats him like a secondary citizen, a dummy, or an intrusion on his or her day. His favorite expression to salespeople is, "I may be crazy, but I'm not stupid." At least he doesn't want to appear stupid.

Guess what? There are a lot of Jacks running around out there. And the sooner you get to know them, the more sales you'll make. Granted, not everybody is like Jack, and the ones who are won't have a label on their forehead reading "Make It Simple for Me and I'll Buy!" Not everybody is alike, some people like to techno-spar, and that's fine. You can probably hold your own with the best of them. Product knowledge, features, and inner-components are probably your strong points.

But one and two syllable words are the "Jack's" of the world's strong point. These people love hearing words like "easy," and "simple." They like phrases like "nothing to it," "plug in and use," and "frees up your time." These are the people who revel in "no assembly required" and "anyone can do it." They like "easy-to-buy," "easy-to-use," and *love* to hear, "you don't have to sit down with an owner's manual for two days." They don't want a customer service number to call; they want to be able to call *you.* They know that customer service representatives put them on hold for days, don't give them the information they want, disconnect them, and are less than friendly. If you can do an end-run around all of these built-up objections, problems, and concerns, you will probably sell Jack in nothing flat. And you won't have to discount either. Jack will be so happy he will refer you to all his other Jack friends, and may even invite you to dinner.

The next time a Jack comes into your store, get to know him (or her) a little bit first. Find out where his technical-info line is. Does he have a VCR, a 35mm camera, and audiocassettes rather than DVDs, a digital camera, or an MP3 player? For the people who like things simple, hide the owner's manual and save the techno-talk. Your product may have bells and whistles that Jack may become comfortable with using once it's in his home, but right now, what's the *main* benefit? What's the *one reason* he's going to love it and should buy right now? Don't talk over his head. Be his friend. Appreciate the fact that his computer on-off switch was hard to find, he threw his palm-pilot away in favor of his paper calendar, and still longs for the days of rotary-dial phones with flashing hold buttons. Support him. Agree with him. And just tell him how much to write the check out for as your product goes out the door or is set up for delivery.

You just have to know Jack.

Is Your Telephone Working in Your Favor?

For years I've talked about how much business you can gain (or lose) from incoming calls. The person who's answering your phone is quarterbacking your business. You might spend a ton of money on advertising, but that interested customer is very apt to make a decision to purchase or not to purchase, strictly on the way they were treated on the phone. But over the years, the statistics have not changed. About 78% of the time, no one asks for the caller's name, and 55% of the time no attempt is made to get a sale or get the caller into the place of business.

Last week I experienced firsthand how nothing has really changed. While the snow was turning into a virtual blizzard, I wanted to do three things: (1) Get some quotes on building/installing a sunroom onto the back of my house; (2) get some prices on buying a new furnace, dehumidifier, and air conditioning system; and (3) get information about gas fireplaces so I could put one on the back porch. I let my fingers do the walking. OK, OK, these are not music stores, but I think you will get the point.

I called and asked the first company about patio enclosures. They spend thousands of dollars each week advertising on TV. The gentleman who answered the phone told me there was no one there right now. It sounded like he was in a hurry, and suggested I call back the next day. He never asked for my name, and he didn't give me any information. So I called another company from the yellow pages. The person who answered told me his name, and asked for mine. He asked for as much information as I could provide, gave me an approximate quote over the phone, and asked if he could come over to give me an exact estimate. He came over, and I spent $13,000 with his company. I never called the first place back. So much for TV advertising.

Next, I called around about furnaces. This was something else. Out of four places I tried, two treated me like an intrusion on their day, one was actually mean when I said I was calling around for estimates, and one very nice person gave me only a very rough estimate. They said they could come over the next day for an exact figure, and told me about the various types of furnaces they sell, and why one was better than the next. They asked for my name and where I lived. I told them. They came over. I spent $4,000. I wonder if those other three places knew how much money they were losing on the phone.

Gas fireplaces were a lesson in futility. I called three places. Nobody asked for my name, and no one tried to get me into their store. None of them had "customer service hours." Here is an actual conversation from one of the places I called:

Me: Hi, do you carry gas fireplaces?
Them: Whatcha need?
Me: A small unit for my sunroom.
Them: C'mon down.
Me: How much do they run?
Them: The prices are all over the lot.
Me: Are you there tonight?
Them: No, we close at 5:30.
Me: Are there any nights you're open?
Them: No.
Me: Why?
Them: Because there are only three of us here, and we put in too much time as it is.
Me: I'll think I'll go someplace else that's more customer-oriented.
Them: Do what you want pal.

That's almost word for word. If they asked for my name, and tried to get me in, even on Saturday morning, I probably would have gone in. Instead, I'm having a contractor make the decision for me, spending a couple of thousand dollars on his choice, which I will make sure is not from the place I called.

Boy, it can be so simple. Businesses, including music stores spend thousands and thousands of dollars on *Yellow Page* advertising, TV and radio spots, and newspaper ads. Then a customer calls to ask about information on a particular instrument, only to be blown away by someone on the phone who doesn't care if the customer comes in or not. It doesn't make sense. Break the cycle. Start by asking for the name of the caller so you can establish a possible prospect. Offer to send them a brochure if it's a high-ticket item, so you can get an address to follow up with. Then try to get the caller to come in and meet you personally. It isn't brain surgery. But if it is so easy, why do only 22% of music stores do it? Beats me.

Do a little soul-searching yourself. How do you handle incoming calls? How about the other people at your store? They're quarterbacking your music business every time the phone rings. Are they NFL-quality or more like second string high school caliber? And how about yourself? Did you get the name of the last person who called? Did you try to get them in to meet you? Could it be time to take your phone skills up a notch?

Simple Ways to Handle Complaining Customers

Customer complaints are a fact of life. No matter how superb our products and services are, there are going to be glitches, mistakes, misunderstandings, and unhappy people. It's a fact of life. It could be over quality, price, service, or the mind-set of the customer. Some complaints can be handled smoothly and easily, and others can reach another level of unhappiness and hostility.

But a customer's complaint or a buyer's dissatisfaction doesn't have to signal the end of a relationship with that customer. Studies have shown that customers whose complaints are handled well are often more loyal to a company than those customers who have never had a problem at all. A customer who complains and has their complaint resolved is more valuable to you than one who is unhappy but never tells you about it. Instead of telling you and letting you correct the problem, they go and tell their neighbors and friends. It becomes a negative PR campaign.

I remember complaining about my cellular phone bill once to one of the major carriers. As you know, cellular phone plans and programs are as complicated and different as airfares. You choose one, and a week later there is a lower price and different program. In this case I was getting overbilled, and receiving dunning letters while the cellular phone company was doing nothing about it. I finally called after the third wrong bill, and started to let the person on the line really have it. After I fired a couple of rounds of hostility at the young lady, I heard nothing. So I reloaded and let her have it all over again. This time she said, "Boy, I don't blame you for getting upset. I would probably feel the same way if I were you." The wind was out of my sails. It was over. I didn't yell anymore. She then said, "I'm not the one who sent you the bill, but I will do everything in my power to correct it." She fixed it, and I was happy.

What you may not realize is you don't have to give away the store to make things right. You don't have to get in a shouting contest with someone whose complaint is unjustified, ludicrous, or stupid. Some people just want to be heard. They just want some type of appeasement, and it isn't always money. In a recent survey, most customers said they wanted the following from store owners, salespeople, and service personnel when they complained.

They wanted to be believed. They wanted someone to see it from their side. They wanted some type of fair settlement, some relief, something to appease them.

If they didn't get the relief they were looking for, they wanted a reasonable explanation of why their requests were denied.

They wanted their complains settled easily and quickly. They didn't want to waste a lot of their time.

They wanted to talk to a minimal number of people. They didn't want to hear "It's not my department," "It's not my job," or "You'll have to talk to someone else." They didn't want to be juggled around and treated like a second-class citizen.

They wanted someone to take responsibility if a mistake was truly made. They wanted to hear, "It's our fault and we will take care of it."

They wanted some sympathy. Buying something that does not meet expectations and having to go back and deal with uncaring store owners or salespeople is not a whole lot of fun. That's why a lot of customers don't come back and complain. They just don't come back, and they tell their friends not to visit you either.

If it is a problem with your store or showroom, and they had a right to complain; they wanted a sincere apology. "Sorry 'bout that" doesn't make it here. It has to be sincere and come from the heart. Put yourself in their shoes. What would you want to hear?

Customers who complain want any number of the above. None of these wishes are unreasonable. Wouldn't it be great if you could make an unhappy customer happy again by treating them civilly and handling their complaint? Even if they were wrong, at least they would tell other people you tried to help them and went out of your way to provide good customer service.

Handling complaints is not an exact science. Each customer is different. Some want to blow off steam and want someone to listen. Others just want an easy fix or settlement. Ignoring these customers or mistreating them, even if they're wrong, is not the answer. Just giving them their money back doesn't always work either. Here's where the "Do unto others" rule should actually be "Do unto others as they want to be done unto." It's simple and it's common sense. And you could gain a lot of repeat business along the way.

Who's Going to Supply the Instruments to These People?

I'd like you to read the article below, and then (if you like it), copy it and hand it to the more mature people who walk into your store. Or maybe you can tape it to a wall where it can be seen? It won't take long. And it will be worth it

Here it is:

HAD A "SENIOR MOMENT RECENTLY"?

Forgetting things like where you left your keys or the name of your colleague's youngest child? Well, the good news is that experiences like these are perfectly normal and no, they don't mean you're getting Alzheimer's. "The signs of early Alzheimer's are typically noticed by other people," explains Lisa D. Ravdin, Ph.D., Director, Cornell Neuropsychology Service, Weill Medical College of Cornell University in New York. "Early Alzheimer's is marked by repetitive speech, forgetting important events, an inability to manage medications, and difficulty finding one's way around familiar places (like getting lost on the way home from the supermarket). If you think you have it, you probably don't."

The bad news, says Dr. Ravdin, is that you can expect more of these kinds of episodes with the passing years. "Unfortunately, a decrease in brain function is inevitable as we age," she explains. "Beginning in our 30s, there are changes in the structure of the brain such as decreased brain weight and volume, and loss of large neurons that result in changes in thinking ability and memory."

If physical changes to the brain are inevitable, and no known agents prevent Alzheimer's disease, is there anything that we can do to keep our wits? Thankfully, the answer is "yes, plenty"—even when it comes to Alzheimer's, a disease whose relentless progress can, even with state-of-the-art treatment, only be delayed, not halted. "The goal is to delay the onset of symptoms," Ravdin says. "Lifestyle changes and enhanced thinking abilities can push back the development of the disease by a few years, resulting in a lower prevalence of the disease as well as decreased economic burden, such as cost of nursing home placement or lost wages for those forced to leave the workforce to care for a loved one."

"There's plenty of evidence that lifestyle choices make a difference," says Ravdin. "Mentally and physically stimulating activities such as *playing a musical instrument,* sports, education, card games, and puzzles build cognitive reserves that protect us from changes in thinking abilities that result from aging or disease." In other words, you can build a buffer against aging and disease so that it takes a greater insult and a longer period of time to see damage. And it's never too late or too early. "Adults of all ages involved in mental and physical activities do better on cognitive tests," Ravdin says. It's not too late to learn to play that musical instrument you always dreamed about. "It just has to be challenging without being frustrating, and most important, you have to enjoy it. Learning a new language might be great mental stimulation but if it frustrates you, or you don't enjoy it, it won't do you any good."

Since many activities will do the trick, you might wonder whether making an effort is really necessary. After all, aren't we continually involved in activities that challenge the brain? From figuring out a new cell phone to making dinner from a new recipe, aren't we continually pushing our brains down new paths? Well, yes—if you're young and active. According to Ravdin, "People's worlds become smaller as they age and they become less engaged in outside life. They lose friends, lose family, and they're not going to work every day. For these people, keeping mentally active requires effort." (Playing a musical instrument with a group develops camaraderie and mental stimulation, plus it can be a lot of fun.)

By the way, the most recent issue of *Esquire* magazine says: "To exercise your brain, learn to play the guitar." Actually any musical instrument will do. So if you're determined to stay sharp, stay active in body and mind. You might not be able to stop the aging process, but you can certainly slow it down. Playing a musical instrument can be just the prescription for a healthier life!

OK, now that this article is going to be copied, handed out, put up on your wall, and sent by e-mail to everyone in your address book, let's think about how to go after this market. What's nice about going after mature adults is that they can take lessons any time during the day (not just after school) and will pay cash for their instrument and anything else you have in the store. They can be encouraged to bring their friends in as well. But here's where it takes a little different turn: Teaching adults is not like teaching kids. It has to be fun. They don't want to be talked down to. And if you put them together playing with other people with the same musical ability, you'll have a continual stream of new customers because they will tell their circle of influence about how much fun they're having and all about their new interest. It's like golf. Few people play golf alone, they play with three others. Those others are usually friends, in the same age group and same station in life. Those older people who play golf have no qualms about dropping $500 for a new driver, $60 a dozen for ProV golf balls, or spending 200 bucks on a new course they never played before. They don't care if they can't break 110; they're having a good time.

Maybe they would like to play a guitar, piano, drums, or even a harmonica? Heck, I'm learning to play electric bass at my age. It works my hands, stretches my fingers, and pushes my brain. I love it. One of my 70-year old golfing buddies just took up guitar. Manufacturers like Yamaha are starting to go after this market as well as some forward-thinking retailers. Everyone else should jump on the bandwagon too. It takes a whole different outlook, you need the right teachers and you need to have a group environment, as well as individual lessons. You also might need a bigger cash register to handle all the money that will be coming in.

How Easy Are You to Reach by E-Mail?

In this age of technology overload, customers can reach us in a variety of ways. We have multi-line telephones, sophisticated answering machines, voice mail, cellular phones, fax machines, e-mail, and interactive websites. Years ago when somebody wanted to reach you, they called your store or house, or sent you a letter. Now they can call you directly on your cellular phone, or send you an e-mail message.

I know you can't be a success at selling if people can't reach you. However, of all the means of communication out there today, I hate e-mail the most. I like to joke that, when I retire, I am going to toss my computer out my second-story office window and never look at e-mail again. I have three e-mail addresses. Some receive less spam than others, but I hate weeding through 40 e-mail advertisements for Viagra prescriptions, body part implants, mortgage loans, debt consolidation, porn sites, and other e-mail junk-of-the-day, just to find a message that has any importance.

Even so, I try to be technologically literate. I use Outlook Express to say when I am away from my computer and to answer e-mail in a timely manner. A few days ago I got an e-mail from Dean Cowdery in St. Louis Park, Minnesota. He liked a column I wrote regarding how a lack of customer service can affect sales. It's nice getting positive feedback about my columns. It wasn't all good though. Dean did have a few suggestions for me. Here is the last part of his e-mail regarding that particular column:

"Perhaps your readers would gain from your insights about who a customer is. In my book it is the vendors, the people who purchase from us, delivery people, etc. I want everyone affiliated with our company to have a good feeling about us.

But, I would like to give a little constructive feedback to you in return for the good article. In attempting to contact you to write this e-mail, I found it extremely difficult to find your e-mail address (as the customer this happens to be my preferred method of communicating with you). After I combed the article, I could only find a telephone number, address, and a web address. Secondly, I visited www.creativeselling.com, but again found no e-mail address or way to e-mail you. Fortunately this web page provided a link (albeit obscure) to your personal website. It was here that I found your e-mail address. This is odd for someone that specializes in the area of selling."

I thought about the letter for a few minutes. Then I thought about it the next day. It started to bother me, so I called him directly to let him know that I don't consider e-mail the most viable medium to reach someone. E-mail is a chore, a bother, a pain in the butt. I guess I'm old. He told me that he uses it as the quickest way to respond to someone. He has a spam filter to get rid of a lot of the junk e-mail, and if I just got with the program and started putting my e-mail address in my columns, it would be a lot easier to get readers to respond. I told him I have my phone number listed in most columns, along with my fax number, and my Bentley-Hall, Inc. web address. That didn't appease him one bit. He said that if you sell anything for a living, you not only need an e-mail address, you need the e-mail address visible so customers don't have to search for it. When they want to send you an e-mail, they want the address at their fingertips. There was nothing I could say to him to combat this line of thought. I gave up and realized he was right.

Customers really want to take the path of least resistance when trying to reach you. Many times that's going to be e-mail.

They don't want to look up your phone number or address, that's why they keep business cards. And what I've learned is you better have an e-mail address and you better make it available. Put it on not only your business cards, but also your invoices, direct mail pieces, and everything else you hand out or send out.

Rotary dial phones with flashing hold buttons are not coming back. E-mail is not going away. Make sure your e-mail address is everywhere your phone number is. Make sure it's everywhere your address is.

Treat e-mail like the alternative communication source that it is. Just remember how important it is in this technologically advanced age. You want your customers to perceive you as easily accessible and readily available. Making your e-mail address available will give this perception. It's a part of customer service you have to remember. E-mail will bring in more business whether you like it or not.

Six Misconceptions When Handling Nasty Customers

Nasty customers are a fact of life. Their Prozac supply runs out and they take it out on you. They were unhappy with their last instrument purchase, and the next thing you know, they're beating up on you. It doesn't matter if you're a rookie or a pro; you could be young or old, male or female. Just look at nasty customers the wrong way, and they'll let you have it with both barrels. Answer their objections to their dissatisfaction, and they'll reload and let you have it again. These are customers who spit and steam, and sometimes, they even use four-letter words. They try to intimidate, love to complain, and may get out of control.

Nasty customers are the ones who say things like:

"You apparently don't know what you're talking about."
"Your competition is *much* cheaper. I'm surprised anybody buys guitars from you."
"It's a wonder you're still in business."
"I never pay sales tax, and I certainly am not going to pay what you ask."
"Where was your last job—McDonald's?"

Nasty customers are worse than tough customers. Tough customers make you earn their business. Nasty customers make you wish you had never crossed their paths. They can be rude, intimidating, manipulative, mean, vulgar, and as many other less-than-complimentary adjectives you can fit in a sentence. Nasty customers come in all ages, sizes, and walks of life. If you never encounter a nasty customer, go on to the next page. If you do have an occasional run-in with Mr. or Ms. Nasty, here are some common misconceptions you might want to think about.

Misconception #1: *The Customer is always right.*
False! Nasty customers may lie. Just because they told you they could get the same instrument a lot cheaper from someone else doesn't mean that they can. They just want to see if they can play with your head, or put you up on the auction block over price. This is the same customer who "used to be in the business," "never pays list," or "doesn't need what you sell." If you know what's right, stick to your guns. Nasty customers can be wrong.

Misconception #2: *Never be ignorant or arrogant.*
Wrong. With nasty, arrogant customers, you can afford to be arrogant as well. You can also be ignorant to their demands. You can be ignorant, or you can be arrogant, but you can't be both at the same time. If you're both, you might turn into a nasty yourself.

Misconception #3: *Customer satisfaction means customer loyalty.*
Bull. Just because nasty customers are satisfied doesn't mean they're coming back. Only loyal customers come back. The trick is to switch that satisfaction to loyalty. But what if you don't want them back? What if they are too much of a hassle to deal with for the few bucks they spend? You decide. You're in control. Handling nasty customers effectively means being in the driver's seat.

Misconception #4: *You get what you give.*
Uh-uh. Nasty customers can be opportunists. Gimmee, gimmee, gimmee. Better terms, lower prices, what more can I have? Give them an inch and they take *two* miles. Don't expect to get back as much as you lay out for a nasty customer. They always want to be one up.

Misconception #5: *Price shoppers always buy on price.*
Nope. They like to think that they are the world's best negotiators. They brag about "buying at cost," "spending less than wholesale," "beating salespeople into the ground," or "getting things thrown in for free." The truth is, nasty customers like to give that impression, even though it's not reality. They will bend when shown that benefits far outweigh the price and that service is a necessity rather than an option. Price shoppers need to hear "no," rather than "OK, I'll take your offer." They will pay your price if their need is great enough. It is up to you to develop that need.

Misconception #6: *Nasty customers are nasty people.*
Sometimes true. Mostly false. All nasty customers have a soft spot somewhere. You have to find it. Get them to smile. Get them to laugh. Say nice things about their mother. Find out if they like flowers. Do they have small children or grandchildren? Do they have a favorite charity? Get them to open up. Get some emotion. Be their friend. It's tough to be nasty to somebody who wants you to like him or her. Forget your product and price list for a minute and concentrate on a little customer rapport.

The funny part about nasty customers is that they usually know they're nasty. It's a part of their personality. Sometimes you have to level out the playing field and not try to beat them at their own game, but to have their game end in a draw. You need them to buy from you and feel good about it at the same time. Don't succumb to a nasty customer. Don't lay down and play dead. Make it a game. Get their money and get a smile out of them at the same time. Make them glad they had a chance to deal with you and your music store. Turn a "whiner" into a "winner" and get a sale at the same time.

Do You Speak the Customer's Language?

All things being equal, customers like to do business with someone they can relate to. If your prices and services are pretty much the same as your competitors', customers are likely to choose to do business with someone they like. They buy on emotion. They shy away from salespeople who annoy or irritate them. It's common sense.

So, how can you relate better to your customers? Speaking and understanding your customers' language is a good place to start. That doesn't mean just Spanish, Korean, Japanese, or any number of recognized languages. It means being able to understand and converse in Southern, jive, hip-hop, adult, cool, senior-citizen, urban, suburban, country, and hundreds of other dialects.

People like people who are like themselves. In other words, if people can relate to you, they will like you. If they like you they will trust you. If they trust you, they are more apt to buy from you.

If your store is in an ethnic section of your city, or if you have a lot of bilingual customers, learning a few words of their native language shows you're trying to be one of them. You don't have to speak fluently. They understand English. Try to understand a few words of their language.

I have a friend who has many Spanish-speaking customers. On his business card, he has the words "El Grande Queso" under his name. That's his title. People who speak Spanish chuckle, and people who don't speak Spanish ask, "What does that mean?" Translated, it means he's the "big cheese." When you get a customer to smile, you're a lot closer to making a sale.

If you're a younger salesperson talking to an older person (that's anyone 10 years older than you), you might want to put yourself in their shoes. Talk in terms they can understand. Don't use the latest slang or overly technical terms. They probably also wouldn't appreciate being called "dude" or even "ma'am."

Someone from New York City has a presence, an attitude, a speech pattern all their own. You have to figure it out for yourself. Same goes with customers from L.A., Minneapolis, Miami, or any other region. You have to adapt to their style. It's called "mirroring."

We've all had customers who want to beat us up verbally so they can buy something for less than it's value, then tell us they'll be back, only to end up buying down the street. Maybe we just haven't spoken their language.

Maybe it's not the price, the service, or the product. Maybe it's us.

Speaking your customers' language doesn't mean taking a three-day Berlitz course. It means talking to them in terms they understand, words they recognize, and phrases they can relate to. If you know all the industry jargon and your customer is an uneducated novice, it's like speaking Portuguese to a Ukrainian.

I remember going shopping for a computer years ago. I didn't know anything about bits, bytes, RAM, or drives. I actually thought "floppy disk" was a stripper from the '50s. I had put off buying a computer for a whole year because I was embarrassed by my ignorance and was worried I wouldn't be able to understand what the salespeople were talking about. I finally bought computer equipment from someone who explained the features and benefits in terms I could understand. Price was not a factor. I was looking for a business whose salespeople would understand my needs, explain things in a language that I could understand, and would put me at ease during the sale.

Don't talk over your customers' heads. Don't be too cool, too clever, or too technical. Know where that fine line is. Talk to your customers in language they'll understand … but first, find out what their language actually is. Everything else will be easy.

Embarrassed a Customer Lately?

I hate shopping for computers. It's worse than shopping for a car. With a car you can get embarrassed because of the haggling and not knowing if you're getting a good deal. With a computer, it's embarrassing not to be completely computer literate, and having someone talk down to you. Techies, who know everything, seem to condescend to those who don't. I'm always afraid the next question I ask will get a "Boy, are you stupid" response. When someone looks at me with that, "I can't believe you asked that question" smirk, I want to turn around and run to the door. Ever happened to you?

My neighbor went out to by a piano the other day. Ended up buying a used one in the paper. She had gone to a local dealer and asked about a piano. The salesperson asked her how much she wanted to spend, and what kind she was looking for. She only wanted to spend a few thousand dollars, and knew nothing about pianos. The salesperson asked if she had any particular make in mind. She only knew the Steinway name and said that's the only make that came to mind. The salesperson said, "Are you crazy? You'd never find a Steinway in *that* price range." She didn't want a Steinway. That's the only name she knew. And she certainly didn't want to do business with someone who thought she was crazy. She left. She was embarrassed.

Have you ever had a customer come into your store who was so misinformed, it was an effort not to laugh? It took all of your control for your jaw *not* to hit the floor at their completely uneducated questions or statements. You might not have said so at the time, but I know you were thinking it. We all have, on occasion. The problem is that even though it might not come out of your mouth, they can still sense it and they get embarrassed. It might not happen all the time … but even once is too much. Here are five things NOT to do to avoid making the customer feel embarrassed:

Don't laugh at them. If they don't know a lot about your instrument and expect it to cost half of what you're selling it for, you're going to have to get them to be your friend before going any further. Be nice. Put yourself in their shoes. How would you feel if you wanted something out of your price range? Explain financing and credit options. Explain features and benefits—*why* it costs what it does. Give them a little education like a good neighbor. Even if they decide not to buy it, they may send other customers to you. You never know.

Don't make the customer feel stupid. Talk in terms they understand. Don't talk over their heads. Stay away from industry jargon they might not be familiar with. Use one and two syllable words, but don't go to the other extreme and start talking in a condescending tone. Your customer could be a neurosurgeon for all you know. So just because she gave you a blank stare when you brought up that digital piano's voicing capability, it doesn't mean she's an idiot. Remember, the more comfortable you can make your customers, the more apt they are to do business with you.

Don't be a jerk. Don't talk about your customer to other salespeople in front of them, as if they weren't there. Saying, "We don't have any beat-up used spinet pianos under $1,000, do we Mike?" Customers who feel they are the salesperson's source of entertainment for the day will seldom buy. And they make sure nobody else will either, guaranteed.

Don't walk away from them like they're not there. OK. They said they just wanted to look. Maybe the last five customers said the same thing and walked out without buying anything. Whose fault was that? Should we take it out on the ones presently in the store? Be courteous and try to engage them in conversation. You never know what might trigger some positive response.

Never judge a customer's station in life buy their looks or their clothes. A customer may look like a panhandler but have thousands of dollars in his pocket and 25 years as a classical pianist. Maybe he drives an old jalopy and has threadbare clothes, but also has a Ph.D. in Music Education and excellent credit. It's easy to think: "He's out of his league." Assume he's not, and make it your business to find out. Look for the silver lining.

One of the problems we have in the music business is that we know a lot. We play. Some of us even have talent. We know the technical side of instruments and love to dazzle customers with our expertise. At least a lot of us do. Nothing can be more fun than talking about a customer after they leave the store. "They wanted a Fender Strat for 200 bucks." "They looked like they couldn't afford a set of strings." "This guy was nuts. I showed him. Told him to go down the street."

Maybe sometimes we have to get it out of our systems. It's when we get it out of our system in front of the customer that's the problem. So hold it in. Smile whether you want to or not. Be polite, be courteous, and don't start with the intimidating, demeaning words and phrases. And don't talk to them as if they have an IQ of 36. Don't embarrass the person doing the buying; it can be an easy thing to do. The hardest part is that sometimes we don't know we're doing it. Be careful. A little tact can go a long way.

CHAPTER 5:
Finding Leads

There's Gold in the Grey Market

Even though I'm older now, I still visit music stores quite often. For one thing, I'm playing more now, even though I've past 60. I have more free time. I also have more money. I like to stop in to see what's new and buy percussion, keyboard accessories, recording equipment, gifts for friends who play, or sheet music. Many times I'll buy a musical item on impulse because I think would be fun to have.

I know a lot of people just like me, with cash and disposable income, who sometimes make quick decisions, but for bigger purchases I usually think things through. However, as I get older there are two things I (and people like me) won't do:

1) I will not buy from someone I think is a jerk.
2) I will not buy from someone who doesn't know what they are doing.

Having said that, I realize everything is in the mind of the beholder. I know I have some quirks, but a lot of people my age have the same quirks. A lot of people my age have the same sentiments as I do—they just don't voice them. They simply don't buy and won't come back.

People in my age group spend a lot more money with salespeople who we think truly know their business. We buy more from people who like their job, who have some personality, and who make us feel good. Since I am a serious customer (who just happens to be way past middle age) with serious money to spend, here are a few of my personal likes and dislikes when I come into your store:

1) I don't want to be called a "senior citizen" ("mature adult" is better).
2) Don't refer to me as "that grey-haired guy." I think my hair is still light brown. I don't remember it changing. Please don't remind me.
3) You don't have to call me "Mr. Popyk." "Bob" is fine with me. I like to buy from people I respect, but I want you to be a friend too.
4) Don't wear a hat in the store. That shows no respect, and if you have one on, I will think you are bald. If it's on backwards, I will ask you if you checked the instructions before putting it on.
5) If I ask you a question, don't read to me from literature or from the side of the box. I can read. My mom taught me when I was five.
6) Ask me what type of music I like first. Kid Rock's latest hit will probably not be my first choice, but it's not going to be Classic '40s either.

7) If the T-shirt you're wearing has a creative use of the "F" word, I will probably not buy from you.

8) If your tattoos and body piercings are taken to a new level, you will probably gross me out and I will look for another salesperson. I will also wonder what the loan officer at your bank will think when you come in for a mortgage or a loan. But, hey, that's just my generation.

9) Have a good attitude. Be your best at all times. Don't tell me you'd rather be out playing, or working someplace else. Believe in yourself and your store.

10) Ask me some engaging questions. Try to get to know me a little bit. Don't use those closes on me. Just look for a need and try to fill it. Be nice. Ask me to buy.

Now if you have taken offense to any of this, I am sorry. However, I also don't care. The nicest part of being older, with more time and more money, is that we can buy where and when we want. Don't think for a minute we are in the minority. People in our age bracket are living longer than ever before, and our segment of the buying population is larger than ever.

Here's a couple of secrets on selling us "old timers" (call us that and we will probably whack you on the side of your head with the nearest music stand).

First, "give without the expectation of getting." Don't try to "sell" us, just help us buy. This is the hardest thing for a salesperson to do with older people, but it's an important key to getting high-level acceptance with mature adults. We know the tricks and the BS, so save it for the less-savvy younger customers. With us, be genuine. Remember, "the more you give, the more you get."

Second, position yourself as a resource. When you give us value with your knowledge and expertise, and you provide information beyond what you are provided with, you will be recommended, sought after, referred, and spoken of highly, to all of the other people we know. We talk. We have friends our age. If you understand us, we will get you more customers than you can imagine. If we like you, we will tell everyone we know. If we don't, we will tell even more.

Where's Your Next Customer Coming From?

If you've been in the music business for any length of time, you've probably noticed that, every once in a while, things start to get a little slow. It's not gangbusters every day of the week, every week of the year. Maybe it's the weather, the economy, vacations, the season, or any number of variables that can affect sales revenue. So, what do you do when business starts to soften? Come up with a new promotion? Run some advertising? Do a mailing campaign?

Great, but these ideas are only good if they actually click and don't cost more than you bring in. If your sales start to go into "tilt" and you don't have a hefty advertising budget, times could get a little tough. There is some marketing you can do however, without spending serious cash. How about looking to your staff for some ideas or talking to your salespeople, or even your administrative personnel, about their thoughts for finding more customers? Could they be of any help? It might not be a bad idea to have a meeting with everyone in your store to ask for their input. See if they have any ideas on how you can get more people to walk through your door. You might be amazed when the lowest paid person on your payroll comes up with an idea or two.

Of course, a lot depends on what type of music store you have (full line, band instruments, combo, pianos, etc.) and whether you have commissioned salespeople. Seven-dollar-an-hour clerks might come up with a few ideas, but after that, they probably will leave it up to you to get more floor traffic. On the other hand, if you have salespeople who work on any type of commission, it definitely will be in their best interest to get everyone involved in creating more customers.

I truly believe that a music store with proactive salespeople, who can help bring customers through the door without relying on media advertising or store promotion, can run rings around competition that is slashing prices and running its third annual "Going Out of Business Sale." It's OK to be reactive and wait for the next customer to come through the door, but how much more gross sales could you be generating if your salespeople could bring their own people?

Generating traffic without a huge ad budget is possible. Car dealers and insurance agencies do it all the time. Real estate people do it, too. Here are my thoughts on a few things you and your salespeople can do to generate more business on their own:

1) Make every incoming phone call count. When someone calls looking

for information about a musical instrument, get their name before giving a price. Use their name during the conversation. It's easy. Just say "This is (your name), who'm I speaking with?" Then try to get them into the store. Put them on your mailing list. Stay in touch with them.

2) Business cards, put to use, can bring in business. Everyone in your store should have their own cards. Invent titles for your employees if you have to. Make sure they have cards with them at all times to give out to their circle of influence—anywhere, anytime. Tell your employees to use them at parties, standing in line at the grocery store, at public events—anywhere they might talk with others. Besides, business cards help give your people pride in where they work.

3) Personal promotion is important. Commissioned salespeople should send out a few notes or postcards each day to past customers urging them to stop by and see them personally about a new item. The card could say something as simple as, "Trying to reach you; give me a call." Ten cards a day is a good target, and the process will only take a few minutes.

4) Make cold calls. If sending out cards is too much, salespeople should call some of their friends, relatives, acquaintances, past customers, new customers, or prospective customers each day. A half a dozen calls a day ought to do it. Tell them about a new instrument that just came that you'd like to get their opinion on. You will be amazed how many people like to

give their opinion, and how many will come into the store to do it. These calls could be made first thing in the morning. If the caller gets an answering machine, you might leave a message saying, "This is (salesperson's name) at (your music store). I've got good news for you. Please give me a call." Everyone likes "good news"—your news could be a special price on a new instrument, or anything that might trigger response.

5) Use your e-mail account. All salespeople should have their own e-mail address list of personal contacts who are interested in music. Have each salesperson come up with some interesting data about the instruments you carry and send out an interesting fact or two each week to their list. An urgency at the end about why the prospect should come to the store ("Limited Time Offer," "Only One Remaining," etc.) is a good idea.

No More Slow Days

If you have a mega-store chain with lots of outlets and someone in charge of marketing and promotion, this column won't mean a whole lot to you. But if you have only one or two stores, with no designated advertising manager, and your advertising and promotions budget isn't in the high-six or seven figure range, you might possibly get an idea or two.

I've always been a big purveyor of what other industries do to bring customers in the door. The real estate, automobile, and insurance guys are very good at finding people to talk to. It's amazing the lengths some salespeople will go to find customers or get traffic in the door. However, the music industry is not exactly a "lead and follow up" business. It's more like a half-clerk/half-salesperson biz with a direct correlation to how much ambition someone has. It also depends on what your music store sells. Keyboard stores are different than combo stores, who are different from band instrument dealers or sound reinforcement specialists. Through the years I have found hundreds of ways to find customers without relying on advertising or promotion. Some work better than others. Not everything works for everybody. And it also depends how much you want (or need) the business and how much you are willing to exert yourself.

About 25 years ago, when I first made the transition between music retail and Bentley-Hall, I would occasionally work with a music dealer who was having a tough time and needed a serious influx of business just to survive. It was a challenge just to see if I could come up with something that would click, even if it was just a short-term solution. Some ideas didn't work, but many did. Working in the trenches back then and coming up with ideas that bought in more customers and created more revenue, gave me a great bank of information for writing and speaking about it over the years.

I remember in the early eighties, a dealer called me from California. His full-line music business was having its ups and downs, and right then it was spinning downward. He was stretched out to his credit limit with suppliers, behind in his sales tax, delinquent with his local advertising agency, and wasn't even sure if he could keep making payroll. I think he put my fee on his mother's credit card. I had some doubts whether anything could be done at that point. When I got out there I found a good-looking store with decent inventory and employees with crappy attitudes. Not only did they think business was bad, they thought it was going to get worse. Nobody was coming in the door. The economy was down, things were slow, there was a lack of interest in musical instruments in their area, and any business that did exist was done by competition that was giving stuff away. You could take the excuses you liked the best. I had to come up with a couple of ideas quick, or I was going to start believing it myself.

I didn't do anything radical. Nothing that other retailers hadn't done in desperation one time or another. I had them paper the windows with holes cut out so there was limited view of the interior of the store. The words, "THREE-DAY GOING OUT FOR BUSINESS SALE" appeared all over the place. This was no time for an ethics course; they were going out for business the three days I was there. I made sure of it. We got helium balloons and had them all over the place. Since the only venue they could advertise was the crawl at the bottom of the cable guide station on TV, we had signs reading "THIS IS THE SALE YOU HEARD ABOUT ON TV!"

At that point I got hold of their past customer list. There were thousands and thousands of names, addresses and phone numbers. There was no money to mail these people, and there was no way the local papers were going to give them any advertising credit. The owner of the store let the salespeople know their jobs were at stake, and it was up to them to help bring in customers that weekend. They divided up the customer list and started calling two days before the sale. They called everybody. They told people this was the biggest sale in their history. If they got an answering machine they left a message: "I've got good news for you, give me a call." People who called back were offered a set of guitar strings, a t-shirt, or a music book for stopping in, depending on what type of customer they were. That was the "good news."

Four thousand flyers were made up and distributed to anyone who would take one. I found a local promotion company who set up a searchlight in front of the store, in trade for a low-priced guitar. We put up a flashing changeable-letter sign in front of the store with also the words: "This is the sale you heard about on TV." There were signs all over the place urging immediate action. It LOOKED like something was going on. Desperate times called for desperate measures. The salespeople got pumped. The adrenaline started to mount. The customers started coming through the door. And after the last sale was made and the last customer left, the salespeople looked at each other and said "Why didn't we do this before?" They did a ton of business. A ton of profitable business.

It wasn't because they couldn't do it before. It was more because they didn't want to. They survived because of desperation and hard work. And it took total involvement with all the salespeople pulling their own weight. The music business is a fun business. The more money you make, the more fun it is.

Are You Selling "Easy-To-Play"?

Recently, *USA Today* ran an article about a day in the life of a Transportation Security Administration screener at one of the nation's busiest airports. Most of the report was pretty predictable. The screener talked about confiscating small knives and lighters, about passengers' short tempers, and so on.

The report also noted that when you spend eight-plus hours a day standing watch at an airport security checkpoint, you learn a few things about the traveling public. For instance, you learn that:

- The condition of passengers' socks is, for the most part, not bad.
- Passengers are much more malleable once they understand what's going on.
- A surprising number are packing harmonicas.

As music store owners, we can learn a lot from that survey. First of all, most people seem to take some pride in themselves, even if it is just clean clothes. Secondly, if you can spend a little more time educating your customers, it's easier to deal with them and sell to them. Finally, more people are interested in music than we realize. We just have to find them if we want our industry to grow.

Let's look at that harmonica thing. Do you have harmonicas at your front register? Do you have harmonica learn-to-play books, CDs, and DVDs? Do you have any other impulse buy, easy-to-play instruments at the front counter?

I talked with one of my friends who owns a piano store in the Southwest. He told me that he sells pianos, organs, and electronic keyboards. But he also sells harmonicas in three price ranges—inexpensive, moderately priced, and slightly expensive.

At Christmas people buy harmonicas by the handful. They buy the "learn-to-play" stuff too. He doesn't want potential customers going to discount stores or bookstores to buy these things. During the rest of the year harmonicas still go out the door, and he said it helps pay the rent. Amazing. I just didn't realize there was that much interest in harmonicas. I don't know if it is because they are easy-to-play, fun, or a way to entertain ourselves and other people. Maybe playing the harmonica is a musical accomplishment people can take a little pride in. (Here's that "pride in ourselves" thing, like the clean socks.)

Whatever the case, it seems that there might be more people out there interested in music than we imagine. Our job is to get them in the store.

I called Mickey Faulhaber at Ward-Brodt Music in Madison, Wisconsin, and asked him how many harmonicas he sells a month. He said, "I don't think it's that many ... let me look." He went to his computer and said, "Oh, here it is—around 50 a month." That's more than 500 so far this year! Jeepers, that is a lot!

Now here's where I get on my soapbox and state a belief I've had for the past 40 years: The more people you get coming through your door, the better your chance for more instrument sales. I also feel it doesn't make any difference how you get them through your door. It could be private lessons, group lessons, print music, music accessories, music gifts, musical tchotchkes, T-shirts with music-related text or logos, inexpensive guitars, low-price, mass-market keyboards, harmonicas, or whatever.

This industry needs more people who show an interest in music to come in our stores, and it's up to us to develop that interest. The mature adult market is underserved. The hobbyists are sometimes overlooked. (I bet a lot of those confiscated harmonicas weren't bought in music stores.) We have to do whatever it takes to get them in OUR store.

"Whatever it takes" is where these ideas start to fall down. Not everyone will do "whatever it takes." Some music stores don't want to deal with educating a consumer. It's a lot easier to have a customer say, "I want that one over there—how much?" than for you to say, "Let me show you all the details about this instrument and how much fun playing it can be."

But "easy-to-play" sells. Check out Herrington catalog. Herrington is not a musical instrument company. It's more like a "fun stuff for adults" company. On the back page is an ad for a Fretlight® guitar, selling at more than $500. (The frets light up to show you where to put your fingers.) Other companies are getting into the game, recognizing that adults will learn to play an instrument if there is an easy way to do it. Let's head them off at the pass.

I can come up with a lot of ideas to get more people into your store, the problem is do you and your salespeople *want* to do it?

I watched a video the other day called Mesmerizing Magic. It was a magician from England explaining how to do some very clever magic tricks. (I'm old, and this sort of thing appeals to me.) He said, "I'm going to show you how to do a lot of tricks. You won't like every trick, and there are some you will have no interest in at all. The idea is to take the ones you really like—the ones that will hold your interest—and do them often enough so you will be able to do them effortlessly. The others you will not be good at because of lack of interest, so forget about them. To be good at them, you have to want to do them."

If you *want* to do something bad enough, you'll figure it out. (By the way, the number of mature adults who are currently learning magic has doubled in the past five years. I bet these people might want to learn to play an instrument as well.)

Are You Depending on Walk-in Traffic as Your Main Source of Sale?

Just about the time that I think the music business is totally different than any other industry, I get a revelation or two that sets my head spinning the other way.

A couple of months ago, I got a call from a car salesman who reads the publication we do for Buick each month. It's called *Buick Creative Selling®* and contains articles on what's working for Buick dealers around the country, plus ideas for making salespeople more productive and ways to crank out more business for the dealership.

This gentleman on the phone told me that last year he sold more than 350 cars, and wanted to know if we'd like to use some of his ideas in our newsletters.

Three hundred and fifty cars a year is a lot of iron by any stretch of the imagination. It's almost one a day ... actually it's more than one a day, because they aren't open Sundays or holidays. That also would mean he would have to earn in excess of $120,000 per year, which is not bad pay for a guy working the floor of a car dealership.

But I don't believe everything I hear anymore. I know piano salespeople who say they sell more than $800,000 gross volume themselves, but they count all the deals they didn't get financed, plus the trade portion at an unrealistic value, plus all the "wish tickets" they're still holding onto.

The same goes for the guy who says he sells incredible numbers of guitars and drums at fantastic margins, but he still drives around in a '83 Plymouth. Some things just don't jive.

Well, before I took this car sales-pro at face value, I decided I'd check him out. So I called his competitor in the same city and asked if he knew this whiz. The answer came back in a flash. "Do I know him? Absolutely. This guy is nuts. I wouldn't want him on my floor. He can't close. He's terrible."

"Wait a minute, wait a minute" I stammered, unable to contain myself. "This guy says he sold more than 350 cars last year." At which point the car competitor said, "Well, yeah, he probably sold that many, but to do it he had to talk to 3,500 people. You see, he talks to everybody, everywhere. He doesn't care. He's continually sending out cards to people he doesn't know, he strikes up conversations with people who are complete strangers, and he asks everybody if they want to buy a car. He's a real loony."

After that little scenario on the phone with his chief competitor, I couldn't wait to get Mr. "Loony" into our office. This 350-car-a-year hammer is as sharp as a razor blade, slicker than whale waste on an iceberg, and he doesn't rely on walk-in traffic to sell cars. We used three of his articles last month. And there are more guys like him around the country. There are some salespeople who are masters at finding customers without relying on advertising or walk-ins.

Which brings me to my friend Brian. Brian owns a guitar store in the Northeast. He has been in business for 16 years. He started when he was 19 years old and now has 10 employees. Brian feels that you should be able to make a living in the music business without relying on walk-in traffic. He does a heck of a job.

I talked to Brian on the phone a few weeks ago and asked him about his secrets for finding customers. What I found out were the not-so-secret secrets that everybody knows, but few take advantage of.

First of all, Brian asks every salesperson he interviews one simple question. "Could you make a living here without relying on walk-in traffic?" A negative answer does nothing to better your chances of a sales job at his store.

Brian keeps in touch with all of his customers on a regular basis. He has a thing about remembering customers' names. He sends out birthday cards, acknowledges weddings, doesn't forget a get-well card, and sometimes will send a gift if the occasion calls for it and it's an important customer.

His store has more than 15,000 customer names on a mailing list, and Brian says he knows at least 4,000 of those people individually. Every customer gets a thank-you note about two weeks after a purchase, and then gets a personal follow-up call two to three weeks later. That call is just to see if everything is OK, and if there are any questions or problems that can be taken care of.

"Rectifying a problem can produce more business if handled promptly," Brian says. "Many people are surprised to find that we care enough to check.

"They tell their friends about us, and their friends become customers. When we correct a problem, or just call to see how a customer is doing, we always ask the customer, 'what's next?' We want to find out what they might need or might be dreaming about. We then follow up again three weeks later."

Constant customer contact is a critical part of their sales program. Brian has salespeople and office staff calling all day on the phone, particularly during the slower periods. One of the problems, according to Brian, is that most people are only home in the evening. A simple but often overlooked point is to get a day phone number for your customer, as well as a home phone. This way you don't end up with no answer or an answering machine.

Brian feels that making the customer your friend is one of the most important parts of making a sale. His staff tries to stay away from greeting new customers with the customary, "Can I help you?" Instead, someone trying out a new guitar might be asked, "Do you play in an area band?" Many times that gets the conversation off to a good start.

It's also important to know your customers financially. Know their spending capabilities. When a new product comes in, a prospect is a better prospect if he is financially able to buy. You also should know whom to target on your mailing list.

Brian says that referrals are big business. Finding out who a satisfied customer's friends are can give you all kinds of sources for leads, and leads produce prospects who produce sales.

What would your sales staff do if you told them tomorrow morning that for the next 90 days there would be no display ads, no classified ads, no radio or television advertising, and they wouldn't be taking "ups"? Could they make a living finding customers on their own, or would they be collecting food stamps?

If your salespeople take time to read the newspaper, do the crossword puzzle, or huddle in circles talking about how bad business is, it might be time to come up with a do-it-yourself program for finding customers.

Customers for musical instruments are wishers and dreamers. It's up to us to make those dreams reality. Constant contact, going that extra step, and talking to everybody about music might bring a lot more business into your store.

But then again, you could always run an ad that says "Pianos 40% Off!" or "Guitars Half Price!" I guess it's up to you.

Bringing Children into Music the Easy Way

I've been carrying around an article from *USA Today's* October 17th edition for quite awhile. The title was "Children Are Ready to Play—Music, That Is." The article talks about expensive musical toys and reads:

"In Toyland, this may literally be the year that sings. And plays guitar. And rocks out. When Toys "R" Us released its annual toy trends list for the season, rock star kids were at the top of its list. Or at least, wannabe rock stars. The musical drivers for tweens, tykes, and infants are everywhere. First: the iPod. The portable music device and its rivals are fueling interest in music. 'There's more music in kids' lives because technology has made it easier to carry around,' says Cliff Annicelli, editor of *Playthings* magazine.

"Big media influences, such as Fox's *American Idol* and Disney's *High School Musical* and *Hannah Montana* are taking over the toy aisle. Dominant video games such as *Guitar Hero* are pushing the beat. Then there are all those parents with keyboards and guitars in the attic—eager to nudge their kids to musical glories they never quite achieved. 'Music is everywhere this year,'" says Bob Giampietro, senior vice president of trends and innovation at Toys "R" Us. "It's a way for parents and grandparents to engage with kids in a way that's very different from baseball, football, and soccer.

"For toy folks, it's big money. Some musical toys sell for over $100. Sales of musical toys could pass $1 billion this season," projects Jim Silver, editor in chief of *Toy Wishes*, a family shopping guide. "For the toy industry there's another big plus: older kids they've been losing may be returning for musical toys."

Man, if the toy industry thinks that the music business is hot, what does that mean for music retailers? For years parents have been telling their children to get away from the TV, video games, and computers and go outside and play. If they're going to play with a $100 plus toy, that possibly might encourage them to get a little more serious about learning to play an instrument; this could really help get more customers into your store.

I think, rather than turning down your nose at these pseudo-instruments, maybe you could stock the high priced ones yourself, just as an impulse item to get more floor traffic. Or maybe occasionally running an ad that you would take any of these higher-priced toys in trade towards the real thing. I bet there are a lot of homes in America right now with an inexpensive keyboard or a big box store guitar in a closet or under a bed—something that was bought at a discount store rather than a music store. And I bet many of these would still be played if lessons had been part of the mix when they were purchased. Lessons and hand-holding are part of *our* business, not discount/toy/big-box stores. If the new generation of musical toys can instill any kind of desire to learn to play on a legitimate instrument, then our industry can really stand to benefit.

One particular toy that got my interest was Mattel's "I Can Play Guitar," which targets kids ages six and up. The guitar plugs into a TV and uses video and a color-coded system to teach kids to play. Would kids who get one of these as a gift want to play a real guitar shortly after mastering the toy? Interesting thought, isn't it?

How Much of This Market Are You Missing?

Over the past few weeks I have felt like a second-class citizen when it comes to learning to play. I will try to explain how people like me are slighted in music stores; but first, let me give you my demographics: I am in my 60s, feel like I'm 40, have some free time, have a couple of bucks saved up, not a whole lot of bills—kids who are grown and on their own—and I have a lot of friends who are like me, looking for fun things to do. We look for interesting/new things to try, and we find new experiences to share. We go on cruises, try new hobbies, and play golf.

My neighbor, Joe, doesn't play golf, so he thought he'd learn to play a musical instrument. He called a few music stores last year that didn't have teachers available during the day, and they kind of talked him out of trying to learn to play because of his age. He settled on garden trains for a hobby instead, because (as he put it), "you get to go to meetings every week, share the same enthusiasm, and talk about your hobby." He told me I should do the same.

Frankly, I thought he gave up a little too easily about learning to play an instrument, because lately I have been getting the urge to play something different. I am a keyboard player who always wanted to play electric bass, so I thought that now would be the time to give it a try. How hard can it be? I decided I would call a few music stores, pick up a bass from one that has a teacher I could relate to, use the Peavey amp from my keyboard, and I would be off and running. Not so easy.

At the first music store I called, I asked about lessons in the late morning or early afternoon. They said, "We only teach after school when kids can come." Another store I called said, "We don't have any teachers at our store, but if you come in we will give you a list of phone numbers of all the ones we work with in the area."

I tried another store. I asked about Saturday lessons (they had nothing before 5 p.m. during the week) and the person answering the phone said, "Most of our teachers sleep late on Saturdays because they play out, so you don't want to book anything before noon. Also, they might have a wedding job on Saturday afternoon and cancel a lot." I refused to give up, so I called another store. This gum-chewing adolescent said, "Aren't you a little old? Our bass and guitar teachers are rockers."

Not being one to quit, I finally settled for an independent music studio with many teachers, not affiliated with a music store. My friends at Yamaha helped me get an electric bass. I thought I was set. I was excited. I took my first bass lesson at 4:30. I got there at 4:15 and sat in a small waiting room with several 10 and 11-year-old kids. One mother came over to me and asked if I was an instructor. I told her I was a student. She said, "Really?" and walked away. (The kids just pretended I wasn't there).

My teacher was a young man, much younger than my youngest daughter. He asked me what I wanted to accomplish. I told him, "I want to play bass well enough to play with a country group within the next 90 days ... maybe back up Toby Keith." That didn't seem to faze him at all, and he asked (get this) "What bass players do you know, or have you heard of?" I told him that I knew Charlie Mingus, Trigger Alpert, and Mike Huckabee. He said he hadn't heard of any of them, whereby I told him to check the paper because the last one is running for president.

Actually, my teacher was a very congenial, talented young man who taught music in one of the public schools during the day. He seemed to be able to put up with my sense of humor and he also played incredibly well. That, of course, made me very nervous. I don't want to look stupid in front of someone 40 years younger than me.

When I got home my buddies asked me how I did. I answered, "Not really well, but I will figure out the mechanics of playing the bass no matter how long it takes me. I lack dexterity and coordination and hate having someone much younger talk down to me." (That's not your first finger, that's your thumb ... think about it and try it again ... Your pointer finger is your first finger.) Telling my friends of my experience did not seem to make them want to jump on the bandwagon and learn a musical instrument themselves.

Now, here is where the story takes a little different turn. I ran into one of my older friends, Bob Piorun, an American Federation of Musicians union musician and teacher. He says he teaches adults, and instead of a half-hour lesson, he teaches four pupils with different instruments for two hours in the morning, and gets them playing together.

Bob has his own book on how to play electric bass, for adults. He wrote one for guitar as well. He is trying to find an opening for me. He is not affiliated with any music store. I told him it was a good thing that he wasn't, because they wouldn't be able to keep enough instruments in stock to keep up with the demand of him teaching the adult market. He even gets a government grant to do adult classes in the evenings at the local museum. Students can come for free. Have you ever thought about this market? Do you even care about adults wanting to play for fun? Us older mature adults are not going away. Our market segment keeps growing by leaps and bounds.

I live in an area where there is about a 250,000 shopping population. There are a lot of music stores here. And in this radius there are A LOT of older people like myself who would like to play a new instrument, another instrument, or any kind of instrument. However, everyone seems to be after the kids, the rockers, and the school band members. Maybe I just didn't find the right store?

Have you ever thought about classes for adults? Do you have special lesson sessions during the day with an instrument to rent to see if the adult likes it? Do you talk about all the medical benefits of learning to play? Do you mention how learning to play a musical instrument can sharpen your memory? (I figure once I learn to play all the scales on my bass, it will be easier to find my keys in the morning).

I am starting with the new teacher, but I may still keep the same local teacher too because if I do a good job I get a free juice box after my lesson. I will also help him get more adult students since he has a program for people like me. Imagine, being able to play with other people like myself, just after a few lessons! People over the age of 15. Even 50 and 60 year olds. How cool is that? We are a great market to go after. And I will learn to play even if Toby Keith doesn't want me. (It's just root-fifth you know).

The Main Ingredient for Increasing Sales

Think about this for a minute: What do Mormons, Jehovah's Witnesses, Amway salespeople, and Mary Kay representatives who drive pink Cadillacs have in common?

Give up? The answer is "an unshakeable belief." They talk about what they believe in all the time. They're sold on it. They're happy to get into a conversation about their beliefs with anybody, anytime. You just can't sway their thinking. Not that there's anything wrong with that. But just question their beliefs or their products, and they'll give you reasons, answers, and product information for as long as you'd like to listen. These people love sharing their beliefs with others. They believe it, and they'd like you to believe it as well.

Same thing goes for salespeople who sell Steinway pianos, Mercedes-Benz automobiles, Rolex watches, or Franklin planners. You are not going to convince these people that there is a better product out there. It just won't happen, so save your breath.

Now, with all that being said, wouldn't this kind of belief in your product make a definite difference in presenting to customers? If you're the dealer, do you truly believe that what you sell is the best made product, or the best product for the money, or the most technically advanced, or the absolute best product to fill your customer's need? If you're the salesperson, do you get excited when you show it? Do you get an adrenaline rush when you explain features and benefits?

A friend of mine works for a national insurance company. He does okay. He was explaining a policy to me that's earning him some decent commissions. He said, "I can beat anybody's plan on this. It's a great policy. I can run circles around the other insurance programs ... except for maybe ABC Company ... and XYZ, Inc." And that's what separates the big-hitters from the also-rans. He just doesn't have that fire built up inside of him to think that his insurance company is absolutely, without a doubt, the very best.

I decided to replace my garage door opener last week. I called around looking for prices. I had almost decided to go with one company; their prices were a little higher, but I thought they had the most to offer. Then I asked the salesperson on the phone why I shouldn't just buy from Sears and install it myself. (I had no intention of doing this ... I don't even know which end of a screwdriver to use, but I just wanted to see what he'd say.) He said, "Well heck, you could do that and pay about half." I hung up and called the next company in the *Yellow Pages*.

Another friend of mine sells digital keyboards. He loves what he does. He gets so excited demonstrating them that he can't wait to tell you about it. He loves to say "This is so great, you're just not going to believe it. Watch! Listen! Let me show you!" His vocabulary is punctuated with superlatives and exclamation points and his own special emphasis. Victor Borge would have loved him. His sales increase every month. He does well year after year, and with an attitude like that, it's no wonder.

I recently took my car in for a simple oil and lube. I went looking around the showroom while it was being done. The salesperson who sold me the car a year ago came over; I told him that I might trade in one of my cars for the new SUV, since it has the expanded, updated OnStar feature that can't be retro-fitted into older models. I explained that we work with On-Star. He knows we work with the car manufacturer. They are one of our biggest clients. He began telling me that the new models aren't selling well, that there's no competitive lease deal right now, and "that OnStar thing is expensive if you don't use it." Not exactly what I wanted to hear. It almost forced me to keep what I have.

The idea here is that you and your salespeople want to be so excited and entrenched in belief that nothing will come in the way of your thinking— not the competitive manufacturers, not the customer, not other salespeople. Try telling a Girl Scout you don't like her cookies, and she'll probably cry. Everybody likes Girl Scout cookies. It's un-American not to buy them. Girl Scouts believe it. They think you should too. When they come to your door, they know it's not a question of whether you're going to buy them—it's a question of which ones and how many? If a customer comes into your store looking at your product, do you already assume they would be crazy not to get it? Is it just a question of model or color?

You need unshakeable belief in what your selling, faith in yourself, and enthusiasm for the business. Belief is the main ingredient. It will weather a bad stock market, a downturn in the economy, and any type of business fluctuations. The easiest way to increase sales is to sell what you really believe in. You become unstoppable. You will talk about it to all your customers, your friends, and at every cocktail party you ever go to. Enthusiasm coupled with belief may not move mountains, but it can move margins upward. So here's my thought: If you're not selling something you truly believe in, find something else to sell. Selling something you can't stand behind becomes a job. Selling a product you believe in is like riding a bicycle downhill. No effort. And lots of fun, too.

First You Have to Get Their Attention

How did your last direct mail piece do? When you sent out your last mailer or flier, how much response did you get? Did your customer, prospect, or addressee actually open your envelope to read your print piece? Think about this for a minute. What do you do with the mail that comes into your store each morning? Do you sort it standing over a wastebasket? You think to yourself: "junk mail (trash), another letter from Publisher's Clearing House (trash), AOL solicitation (trash), American Express bill (keep), bulk-mail ad piece (trash), personal letter with 42-cent stamp (keep)," and so on? You're not alone. So how do you know those next 100, 500, or 5,000 envelopes you send out promoting your next new product, sales event, or preferred-customer sale are even going to get opened? First you have to get their attention.

I received a direct-mail piece the other day that had on the outside of the envelope the words: "This is not another letter from Ed McMahon." Clever idea. I opened the envelope, read the piece, and then threw it away. But at least I read it first. They had their shot at me. And that's what direct mail is all about. If your prospects or customers don't open the envelope, if they don't read what's inside, you're spinning your wheels. So, how do you get people to give you their attention, even if it's just for a few seconds?

The easiest way to determine what works is to go through your mail in the morning and see what gets your attention. What makes you want to open an envelope? First of all, you may notice that any personal-size envelope with an address written in longhand and a 42-cent stamp gets opened right away. Bulk mail doesn't. Any letter that looks like it might be from one of your friends and not a bill or a solicitation gets opened right away. Postcards get looked at right away, because you don't have to open an envelope. Start to see any similarity? If it looks like junk mail, it probably is junk mail. If it looks important, it probably is. So the idea, I guess, is to make your piece not look like junk mail. Make it look important. Get their attention.

It also depends on how many people you're sending your direct mail piece to. If you are targeting a smaller audience, you probably can spend more and be more creative. Roland Musical Instruments sent a direct mail piece out to their dealers informing them of an upcoming dealer meeting. They wanted to make sure it didn't get lost in the midst of their dealers' other mail that day, so they sent it in the form of a space gun. They actually bought the guns retail and had them customized, printed, and reboxed. The guns were shaped like spaceships and when you pulled the trigger they shot out little foam disks printed with product information. They made a great noise, and the disks flew about 30 feet. The theme was "new-product launch." No one threw them away. Everybody played with them. They caught everybody's attention.

Wood Mode Kitchens sent all of their distributors a compact disc in an envelope informing them of a new sales campaign. On the outside of the envelope were the words: "This CD will self-destruct in five minutes." Everybody played the CD. It got their attention.

One of the more successful car salespeople in the country sends out 10 postcards a day to his past prospects and customers with the words: "Trying to reach you, please give me a call." That simple. Nothing more. It averages an 80% response rate because of people's curiosity as to why they should call. It gets their attention.

A salesperson in a Sea Ray boat dealership tries to get a prospect back in one more time by sending a letter with 21 stamps on it. They are all two-cent stamps. Everyone else sticks 42-cent stamps on their envelopes or runs them through a meter. His letter stands out. It always gets opened.[5]

A well-known copywriter got his newsletter off the ground by sending a letter with a dollar billed taped inside. The next words were, "I want to get you used to receiving money in the mail." It got my attention. I kept the dollar bill and spent $179 to subscribe.

Everyone has received a letter that states, "You may have already won … " but nothing beats, "You have already won!" How badly do you want more people in your store? Can you afford to give away a set of guitar strings, a T-shirt, or something else to do it? Is it worth a few dollars to bring a potential customer in to see you personally? It might get their attention. You might want to try it.

When Do You Stop Following a Lead?

My neighbor is remodeling his bathroom. He and his wife have been thinking about it for years. They're putting in a whirlpool bath, separate shower stall, double sinks, heated towel rods, new vanities, and all kinds of amenities. After that, they start on the kitchen. They've selected some really nice custom cabinets, great looking countertops, state-of-the-art appliances, and a hardwood floor. This is truly the stuff that dreams are made of.

I got curious after I saw truck, after truck pull up, so I went over there and asked what they were doing and who was doing the work. You see, I remember when they started thinking about this five years ago. They had someone come out with plans and estimates from one of the major kitchen and bath centers in town, but then decided to put it off. What amazed me was that, when they finally decided to move on the project, they chose someone else to do the work. I wanted to know why. They said that the salesperson from the showroom they had first visited called them after he gave them the estimates. At that time, they told him that they just couldn't fit it in their budget right then. They didn't have the money. Their kids were going to college. They decided they couldn't afford it. End of story. The guy didn't call back. Didn't keep in touch.

So let's fast-forward to today—five years later. Things change. Their kids are out of college. They inherit a ton of money when a remaining parent passes away. One day, while at a local home show, they get impulsive. They see something they like. They have someone from a different company start with estimates all over again. They start reviewing their options and making style and color selections again, renewing their enthusiasm for getting the work done. They sign a contract and the real fun begins. They completely forgot about the salesperson from five years before. Couldn't even remember his name. Wow. Bet that guy wouldn't like to hear that they're dropping tens of thousands of dollars into a remodeling job he could have had. I mean, *should* have had.

Do you know that on a national average, only 44% of the leads generated from manufacturers, *Yellow Page* advertising, and home shows are ever followed up? Do you know that 22% of the people who are following up on those leads quit after the first "no"? And after that, 14% quit after three "no's"? Then 12% quit after four "no's"? That totals 92%. Now, try to follow me on this, 60% of all kitchen and bath buyers say "no" about four times before they say "yes." So, if 92% of our competition is out of the running after four "no's," this must mean that 8% of the salespeople get 60% of the business just by continuing to ask, by still following up leads—just by being patient, persistent, and keeping in touch.

I know, I know. When people say, "No, we don't have the money," you don't want to keep bugging them. We're all afraid of being perceived as "pests." But how would you know if their finances changed? How long do you keep them in your lead file? How will you know if they move out of state? How will you know when they're ready to do business with you?

And therein lies the secret to creating more business for yourself and your store. You have to call or write those leads once in a while until they buy, die, or move. You have to stay in touch. And that doesn't mean pestering them about buying. It means letting them know when you've come across something new, innovative, less expensive—something that made you think of them, something that would be ideal for their needs. Staying in touch can just be about making casual conversation. See how their kids are doing and if they've begun music lessons, how that vacation on the coast was, and if they've seen anything they would possibly like to discuss. Don't be an obnoxious salesperson. Be a friend. Be a nice person.

If your hot lead suddenly becomes a little refrigerated, first find out what the real reason is. Ask for permission to call back once in a while. To check in if you have something you think would be of interest to them. Maybe they're thinking about purchasing a piano, and they give you that "we'll think about it and get back to you … It's not something we're going to do right now" objection #11357. You say OK, and mention you'll get back to them in a few weeks. They say, "Don't call us, we'll call you." This is not Hollywood. They're probably not going to call you back. What you need to do is ask their permission to give them a call if you find something exciting, more in their price range, different, smaller, larger, whatever. Maybe they're looking at a piano some time in the future. For now, you could call them back to tell them about a new keyboard that just came in.

Maybe you can drop them a note to say "Got good news for you, give me a call." You can do this after a few weeks, a few months, or even after a year. The whole idea is not to let them forget about you. Or else they might just drift down the street, to another showroom, to another salesperson. They are not going to keep your card on their refrigerator with a magnet for the next three years. You'll be lucky if that card stays around for three days.

Something else: When you stay in touch with your prospect, don't be bland, dull, or uncreative on the phone or by letter. Don't be boorish. Don't call to say, "Have you made a decision yet?" If you call, have something genuinely new or different to talk to them about. Throw in a little small talk. Get yourself excited about some new instrument or lesson program so they can get excited too. Stand up while you're on the phone. Move around. Motion creates emotion. Find out if your prospect has any need they didn't tell you about before, and see if you can fill that need. But above all, call back more than once. Write more than once. Don't let your competition grab your prospect or customer, just because you let them go. You're in this business for the long haul. This is not short term. It can be a fun career. And the more business you do, the more money you make, and the more fun it can be.

It starts with following up every lead. And it continues by following those leads up more than just once or twice.

The Incredible Power of Personal Contact

There are many ways to find customers in this day and age. There are the major megabuck media—network television programming, drive time radio, direct mail, and the daily newspapers. Then there are the support groups like billboards, shopper papers, and local origination cable television. And then there's networking.

"Networking" is the buzzword of the '90s. If your salespeople are good at it, your sales will increase, your advertising and promotional expenses will go down, and your competition won't know how you're getting all of your business.

There's a keyboard salesman in Ohio who asked me not to use his name. He'll sell roughly $900,000 worth of pianos, organs, and digital keyboards this year. He has an industrial-size Rolodex, the one that comes with a lock and key that sits on his desk. He doesn't wait for an "up" or for his store to run a special sale.

He's continually calling old customers, keeping in contact with friends who can steer him to new prospects, and finding new people to talk to about keyboard instruments.

The automobile salesman in New York who sells more than 300 cars a year just by utilizing his own networking program never worries about economic conditions or interest rates.

Networking means more than just "who you know." It means what to say, what to ask, and how to go about it. But if you're thinking that it won't work for you because you don't know many people, you could be wrong. You probably know more people than you realize ... sometimes it's just a matter of knowing where to start.

For example, you might want to start with your relatives. And then, how about their relatives? At least you have a common thread—you know the same people. Then there are your friends. Those are the easy people to talk to.

But here are some other people you might add to your "who do you know" list:

Who cuts your hair? Who sold you your watch? Who sells you your suits? Who fixes your television or DVD player? Who takes pictures of your family? Who do you know through your children? Who is your veterinarian? Who are your children's teachers? Who is the loan officer at your bank?

Who sells you office supplies? Who sold you your furniture? Who does your dry cleaning? Who do you play golf or bowl with? Who sold you your house? Who do you know who's buying a new house? Who is expecting a new baby? Who is on your Christmas card list? Who do you write checks to every month? Who is your florist? Who delivers your mail? Who painted your house? Who has a new or growing business?

Who do you know from ... Your old job? School or college? Local civic organizations? Your old neighborhood?

And also who do you know who ... Is a doctor? Is a nurse? Sold you your car? Sells you groceries? Fixes your car? Sold you your glasses? Sells you your shoes? Runs your local theater? Is a dentist? Is your lawyer? Runs your local deli? Is your printer? Are your neighbors? Runs a physical fitness center? Sells you appliances?

Now this is just a start. But if you rack your brain, you can probably double or triple that list. And this is where your networking begins.

The people you do business with have somewhat of an obligation to reciprocate. However, if you just hit them directly with, "Do you want to buy a guitar? (or a set of drums, or a piano, or whatever), you might get an immediate "no." But if you say something like, "I've just started selling musical instruments ... If you were to go into my business tomorrow, who would you talk to?" they're more apt to come up with some names of very viable prospective customers, since you do business with them. Not only that, when the subject of musical instruments comes up at the next PTA meeting or cocktail party, guess whose name they'll probably bring into the conversation? And that's where it starts.

There's more to networking than a onetime shot asking people if they're interested. It's keeping in touch so that when they are interested, they think of you. It's keeping in touch by being interested in their lives so that they are interested in yours.

What happens with your "who do you know" list is that once it's refined and honed down to actual prospects or prospective prospects, it can spin off business like you won't believe. The only problem here is that you have to work at it. And that's what separates the amateurs from the pros. Networking might mean seeing an article in a magazine and sending it to the person you think might be interested. Networking might mean sending postcards to certain people when you're on vacation, so that when you get back, they'll be happy to talk to you ... because you thought of them.

Networking might not only mean letting people know about changes in your business, but being interested enough to care about changes in their business.

Networking might mean taking a picture of the person and sending it to them with a note. It might mean a quick letter, a quick call, or a quick visit. It could be a congratulations for an award, or a birthday greeting.

There was a survey done a couple of years ago in a major office building. Two people in the building were given a book of raffle tickets to sell to other people in the building. The first person was told just to solicit people during the early part of the afternoon. The second person made an initial approach in the morning saying, "I'm going down to get a Coke; Would you like me to get you one, too?" Then in the early part of the afternoon, he asked the same people to buy a raffle ticket.

The end result was that the first person sold only 50% of his raffle tickets, but the second person sold the entire book, and could have probably easily sold another!

Networking. That's all it is. Networking has to be done on a regular, conscientious basis to be effective. A "here today, gone tomorrow" pattern doesn't work. The more people you know, and the more people who think you care, and the more people you stay in touch with *through an organized effort* will have a definite, proportional effect on how much business you're going to do.

Personal contact on a regular basis can increase your sales tremendously. But you have to work at it. Or you can just sit back and wait for people to come in the door. The choice is yours.

How's Your Attitude So Far This Year?

"SLOW SUMMER SALES—Dealers throughout the country are complaining that summer business is dull, trade is listless, and the outlook is discouraging; at least until the Fall when the cooler weather sets in." [From *The Music Trades*, September 1906]

Has this year been any different than business reported in *The Music Trades* 100 years ago? I've heard from a lot of music dealers about business being soft. Some dealers said it was like "shutting off the tap." I don't know how you've faired, but the consensus of opinion is that it's been tough.

Maybe you're one of the lucky music store owners who have been holding their own, but if so, you might be the exception. If you've gone through weeks where outgo is more than income and things get worse after that, what do you do?

Over the years I've found that when biz takes a downturn, you can only do two things: 1) tighten up on expenses, watch your margins, and make the most of existing business; or 2) find more customers.

Now, I'm not a financial guy. I have no expertise in profit-and-loss spreadsheets. I do, however, have a degree in street-smarts from the School of Hard-Knocks. I know what it is to have to scramble for more business. And, after 25 years of working with not only the music industry but the boating, automotive, recreation, cruise, and kitchen & bath industries, I can tell you that everybody has their down periods. The quickest way to bring in more revenue is to find more people to talk to. Come up with any way to get more traffic through the door. In other words, MORE CUSTOMERS = MORE SALES. That's it. It's that simple.

OK, maybe it's not quite that easy, but you can't turn your business around by cutting back expenses alone. In order to increase revenue you need people to talk to. I can come up with hundreds of ideas for music salespeople to create business on their own, but they have got to be put to use. You just can't give these ideas lip service. They have to be put into action on a regular basis.

Once you find something that works, you keep doing it. I don't care if it is clever PR, mailers, personal promotion, referrals, telemarketing, class lessons, or using the Internet. If you have a consistent program and involve your staff, then sales will follow. After that it's up to you to control costs and expenses.

But here's where the problem lies: A bad attitude will start to make your ship go down. Once you start saying that nothing will work, business stinks, making payroll is tough, and customers aren't coming in like they used to, people will agree with you. You become the prophet of your own destiny.

I was talking with Blake Cooper of Cooper Music in Atlanta the other day. He was telling me that it is time for a hard look at expenses and maybe even a new game plan to stay profitable during the tougher times. I concur, but it's also time for an attitude check. I don't know how to do it on cost-cutting and expense-watching alone. It is not my forte. I will however, share the wisdom of Ernie Sposato, former major carpet retailer who was in business during my days in music retail.

Ernie's now in his 80s. I was in my 20s back then. He said, "When things get tough, concentrate on getting more people through the door. You can't turn a looker into a buyer without getting them first through the door. Everything else will take care of itself after that." I never forgot that statement.

After I sold my music stores, I spent the rest of my career coming up with ideas for finding customers, creating more store traffic, and cranking new biz for the retail industry. It's time to shift gears a little bit. Maybe its time to really go after the "boomer consumer" that I've been talking about.

People my age have a lot of discretionary cash and are always looking for a new hobby or something to occupy their brain. If those music hobbyists can get their friends involved as well, it's even twice as appealing. Why not go after us older folks? Just don't let us think we're old!

How about add-ons and accessories? Are you really pushing those full margin items after that $99 guitar is sold? How about used and vintage instruments, on which you can get 50 points or more? How about an outside event where you don't have to give the stuff away?

The mass-market stores and the Internet are never going to go away, so why not hit where they're not? Increase your lesson programs, get some buzz going in town about what you're doing and what you have new, and get your employees involved in bringing in more customers on their own.

And … don't tell people business stinks. Bill Boyce of Piano Distributors in Florida told me that he faxes all of his stores positive reinforcement each week. Here are his exact words from one of his faxes: "Make positive statements but be truthful, like a weatherman who never says 'partly cloudy,' but instead 'partly sunny.' It's all how you word it and say it. Remember to talk positive about your company, your instruments, and YOURSELF! Real estate sales may be down, *but* durable goods sales are up for the first six months this year. That's positive proof retail sales are good."

I agree. No one wants to buy from a place where business is bad. Success breeds success. Try looking the part, even if you have to fake it.

CHAPTER 6:
Self Promotion

The Power of a Name

I was recently waiting for my plane to board at a Northwest gate, when a little boy about three or four years old reached the end of his patience level. He was running all over the place, bouncing off walls, getting underfoot, and causing the general disruption that only kids under five can. His mother kept yelling: "Joshua, don't do that … Joshua, come here this instant … Joshua get off there … Joshua, sit down!"

The plane got ready to board, and Joshua was in the jetway. Sitting down. Standing up. Running around. Sitting down again. I grabbed my carry-ons and started down the jetway. As I passed Joshua I said, "Look out Josh, you're going to get run over." He got up, ran to his mother, and yelled, "MOM, HE KNOWS ME … HE KNOWS MY NAME!" Amazing. Now we were buddies. He waved to me as he passed my seat on the plane.

In the music business, just knowing your customer's name and using it creatively can do wonders for your sales. In direct mail it can get you tremendous results.

If you're using a direct mail campaign for your next promotion, you know that results can be minimal—it's kind of a crap-shoot, depending on the number of pieces, how strong the message is, etc. I know that sometimes we're lucky if we get one-half of 1% response on a mailing. And sometimes those mailings cost a lot. Besides the piece itself, there's the stuffing, sealing, stamping, and sending. Postage rates are high, and response can be low. To reduce costs, we often use the same letter for everyone. It usually begins: "Dear friend," "Dear customer," "Dear music lover," or something else equally bland and generic.

Of course, if the letter was addressed to you personally, and began with "Hi John" (assuming that's your name) you'd probably feel a little differently about it. Or maybe "Dear Mr. Jones," or "We thought this would be perfect for John Jones." It would at least get your attention for a few more seconds. Responses go up dramatically when the direct mail piece has the reader's name at the beginning. People like it when you know their names.

But many music dealers don't have up-to-date mailing lists, sophisticated mail-merge computer programs, or the time or the money to put together individualized, personalized letters. In those cases, there are a couple of things you might try when it's time for your next mailing. For starters, consider sending out a few letters a day that are personalized, rather than generic, to see if using your customer's or prospect's name in the letter increases the pulling power and is worth the extra time and cost.

You could also consider using the same technique a friend of mine in the publishing business uses to grab readers' attention. He sends the same letter to a number of people (maybe 300 or 400 at a time), and in the letter he lists the names of about 100 of his customers. The letter states, "For our best customers, if your name is listed below, you can order the current or new products (whatever he's promoting) at 40% less than the retail price". Or it could be 20%, or any other figure. It depends on the product.

The first thing people do when they read one of these letters is check to see if their names appear on the list. If their names are there, they feel special. They feel honored that he thinks about them as his better customers. He told me that the first time he sent out these letters, he knew it was going to work immediately because people called him to ask why their names weren't on the list. And they wanted to know if they were entitled to the discount. People call him. He sells product.

Sometimes he gets very creative with the list. In his last letter, I noticed my name was between Alfonse D'Amato and Joey Buttafuoco. I guess it was a "New York" list. But generally, he does list his most recent customers, some of his better-known customers, and certainly some of his best customers. He tells me he gets a 15% response rate to these letters, compared to a 1% response when he doesn't list the names.

People love to hear their names. People love to see their names. The more you use them, the more likely you are to get a positive response in a direct-mail campaign. How you do it is up to you. You can roll the dice and spend big bucks with a personalized approach and customized letters to thousands of people. Or you can do a few at a time to see if it works first. Then again, you can be clever and creative to give the appearance of personalization. How you do it doesn't matter. All that matters is whether it works.

You see, direct mail is a "what" medium, not a "why" medium. We know "what" works, but we seldom know "why." We know for a fact that the more personalized a letter is, the better response we'll get. It starts with using the recipient's name on the envelope (never send something to "occupant"). And the name has to be spelled correctly. Then, when you use the person's name in your letter, it really gets the reader's attention. It's a rifle-shot approach to buckshot marketing. It could also give you a bigger bang for your buck!

P.S. The "P.S." is the most important part of your letter. Many times people scan the letter and go right to the P.S. If you personalize the P.S., it's three times as effective. A good postscript can make the recipients want to go back and reread your entire letter. So, if you do have to send a form letter to everyone, you might consider adding a handwritten P.S. to the letters going to your most important customers. The few minutes it takes you to write a sentence by hand to your best customers could pay off big in terms of a better response rate and higher sales.

How Important Are Your Business Cards?

I once wrote a column about how to increase business using something as simple as those little billboards with your name on them—the ones you carry around in your pocket or purse … your business cards. It was all about creative touches like stapling your business card to every check when paying a bill by mail, or clever ideas like not giving your card to a person who asks for it until you're sure he or she didn't ask just to get away from you. Or what to do if you don't have a card with you, but need something better than a cocktail napkin to write your phone number on.

Business cards are both the wave of the future and the way of the past. The cards may be low-tech, but they can leave an indelible impression. Think of the Lone Ranger. With a flurry of hoofs, a cloud of dust, and a hearty "Hi-Yo Silver," the Lone Ranger rides off into the sunset leaving everyone saying, "Who was that masked man?" And what did he leave behind for the people to remember him by? A shotgun shell? A spent .22 caliber cartridge? No. A silver bullet! Something that set him apart from all the rest. So, you've got two choices when handing out your business card. You can hand out a silver bullet in a memorable way, or you can just take a spent shell out of your pocket and hope for the best.

A business card is your signature. It reveals a lot about you. The Lone Ranger didn't carry his silver bullets around in his pocket, getting dirty, scratched and dusty. He kept them in his ammo belt so they always looked brand new. And he always presented a silver bullet in a way that made the recipients proud to accept it. They were happy to receive it. They didn't throw it out. They kept it around. They couldn't wait to show it to their friends.

You don't want to leave potential customers saying, "Who was that masked man?" Make sure they know. Make sure they remember. Make sure they know who you are and what you do. Most importantly, leave an impression so ingrained that they automatically keep you in mind for the future. However, you need more than a good-looking business card to help create more business.

What's more important is the person behind the business card. A jerk with a great looking business card is still a jerk. You need a little personality along with personal contact. You need to work on your schmoozing skills, and you need to capitalize on your own "magic circle" of influence. The more people you talk to, the better your chance of doing more business. Business cards are an integral part of networking.

When someone asks what you do, you have the perfect opportunity to give out a business card. You explain what you do as you hand over your card. Best-selling author Harvey Mackay suggests a multiple choice response to the question, because it gives the other person more than one possible way to connect. He says that his typical answer is something like:

"One, I sell envelopes. Two, I write self-help books. And three, I jog. I'm always looking for ideas for one and two, and trying to figure out how to get paid for number three."

Do you have a unique answer when someone asks what you do? What do you say when you hand out your business card? Come up with something that fits your personality, something that can make an impression. Then all you have to do is start finding more people who you can give your card to.

The next person doesn't necessarily need a musical instrument. Maybe they're not quite interested in the music business. But once you establish a little rapport, get them to be your friends, *and after you find out what they do,* you might just say, "If you were to go into my business tomorrow, who would you talk to?"

And most times you will get a name. Usually it will probably be to get you off their backs. But hey, you might just get a great lead. A super contact. Someone else to give your business card to. And it goes on from there.

If you'd like to read all the ways to use your business card to actually create more business, just go into Border's, Barnes & Noble, or any local bookstore and ask for *Here's My Card.* Or access Amazon.com. Better yet, buy two and give one to a friend.

I'd certainly appreciate it.

The Power of the Word "Only"

You're an expert in the music business; you know musical instruments inside and out. You can explain features and benefits like there's no tomorrow—a master at demonstrating anything the manufacturers can come up with. So if you're not closing as many sales as you like, it probably has nothing to do with your ability to talk about your products or services. It could, however, have everything to do with your ability to talk about yourself.

You see, it doesn't matter how good you are if you're the only one who knows. Think about it: how do you differentiate yourself from your competition? What makes you so special? Do you have a personal 60-second commercial about yourself or your store that sets you apart from everybody else? You should. When somebody says, "Why should I buy from you?" does your response sound like one of the following?

"I've been in business for more than 10 years."
"We've got great service."
"We've got great quality."
"I've got better prices than anybody else around."
"We stand behind every sale."

Big deal. The local car dealer, sporting goods store, or dry cleaner probably says the same thing. How are you *different*?

Does the answering machine at your store simply say, "We're not here to take your call right now, leave your name, number, and a brief message and we'll get back to you"? Well, so does everybody else's. You're missing a great opportunity to insert your own personal commercial in an answering machine or voice mail message. We spend 14 million hours in our lifetime listening to voice mail (OK, that's an exaggeration, but it sure seems like it). Why not capitalize on it? Stand out from your competitors—and not just on the sales floor, but every time you tell someone what you do, every time your answering machine picks up, every time people see you in the paper. So how do you do it, you ask? Use the word "only."

That's it. It's simple. Would you rather go to a heart specialist who has been practicing for more than 20 years, or one who "is the only doctor acknowledged by the Harvard Medical Research Institute as a leading area practitioner?" Which is more attention grabbing: an answering machine message that simply asks for a name and phone number, or one that lets the caller know that you are "the only store that's open evenings" or "the area's only Yamaha Piano dealer?"

What makes you an "only?"

The **ONLY**
Store in town
with...

Are you the *only* guitar dealer/owner in your
city who is actually a professional musician
as well?

Are you the *only* store to receive a specific
award?

Are you the *only* authorized Peavey, Sabian or
Roland dealer for miles around?

Are you the *only* salesperson to receive accredita-
tion of accomplishment from a specific manufacturer?

Are you the *only* exclusive drum and cymbal shop in the state?

I think you get the idea. You can have a lot of "onlys." But if you don't
bring them up, no one will ever know. So practice that 60-second "only"
commercial until you are blue in the face. Practice until you can recite it
without even thinking. This way, when someone at a cocktail party asks
you what you do, you spontaneously say, "I sell pianos at Bob's Music Shop,
we're the *only* ..." Or, "I'm a guitar instructor, the *only* one in the area to
specialize in ..." What a difference.

To stand out from the crowd, you have to be unique. To be unique, you
have to be the *only* one of your kind. It says so in the dictionary. Do a little
soul searching and figure out what keeps you from being a carbon copy of
other stores or salespeople in town. Do a little survey of your customers
and ask why they bought from you.

You might be surprised at what you hear:

You were the *only* store that was open on Sunday.

You were the *only* salesperson who specialized in playing classical music.

You were the *only* salesperson we could ever call at home when we had
a question.

You were the *only* store to offer 60-month financing.

You were the *only* salesperson who took the time to come to our home
to explain the instrument.

Sift through all those "only's," and find the truly relevant ones—pick one
that sets you apart from everyone else. Then capitalize on it. Make it part
of your sales presentation. Make it part of your personal 60-second commercial. Use your "only" on your answering machine, in your ads, and on

your business card. Let the world know. Let it be your signature.

People do business with people they like, and people tend to like the unique, stand-out-from-the-rest, one-of-a-kind type of person. If someone likes you, they'll trust you. If they trust you, they're more inclined to buy from you. Your "only" can make all the difference.

It's Not Who You Know, It's Who Knows You

In the world of selling, the gurus of sales smarts tell us that the easiest way to get immediate business without a lot of hassle is to sell to "our circle of influence." That's our immediate family, our relatives, our friends, our buddies, our neighbors, and the people we come in contact with on a daily basis. This is where the multi-level marketing people tell their down-lines to start looking for business. That's where the Mary Kay cosmetic people are masters at finding others to listen to their pitch. The same goes for the religious groups that recruit on a one-to-one basis.

But that's not enough in the music business. Sure, it's great if your relatives and friends come in and buy an amp, guitar, keyboard, or drumhead from you. It's nice when their kids rent a band instrument, when the time comes. But sooner or later you'll find yourself running out of relatives, and you'll start running out of friends. At that point you can just wait to see who comes in the door, or you can start relying on more advertising to attract new buyers. But if you're operating on a budget and can't afford to be on television every day, or in the paper every week, you and your salespeople might think about "personal advertising" campaigns to keep things rolling.

That's more than your circle of influence. It's not just a matter of who you know, it's who knows you. When people are ready to buy a musical instrument, do they know who you are? Do they know where to go? Do they feel like you're a friend in the business? Personal advertising is more than those little billboards (aka business cards) with your name on them that you carry in your pocket.

Have you ever thought about what you actually do with your business cards? Most salespeople use them when they can't close a sale. It's an easy out for them. They just say, "Here's my card. Stop back and see me if you decide."

You can use business cards in a lot more productive ways.

You could staple them to every check you pay by mail. A human being will have to handle the card, even if it's just to throw it away. At least they'd know of you if they're thinking about buying a musical instrument.

You could leave your card with a tip in a restaurant. Just write: "Bring this card in for a free gift" on the back, and you might find a new customer walking through your door.

Now take a look at your checkbook register. Those are people you do business with month after month. Do they know what you do for a living? Did you ever think about telling them? If you support them and their business, they owe it to you to do the same. All it takes is asking them to mention you and your store to their friends. You could also ask, "Who do you know who might be interested in a musical instrument?"

Now here's the tough part. Expanding your "Who knows you" list means community involvement, networking, and personal contact. Ugh. Who wants to talk about business after the store is closed? There lies the problem. Only the salespeople who really want to do a lot of business capitalize on personal promotion. Tell everyone what you do. Try to get them in to visit you personally. Find out a little about everyone you meet so that you can create enough rapport to bring them in as customers someday. Join the Rotary, Kiwanis, Lions, and any service club where you might fit in. Take part in Little League, Boy Scouts and Girl Scouts, support a local band, and get involved in your church.

Don't do it to promote your business. Do it to promote yourself as a nice person. People like to do business with the people they consider friends. It starts with finding more people to talk to so they can know you. Some people call it networking. It's more like "schmoozing." The best schmoozer always ends up with the best circle of business friends.

That doesn't even mean you have to talk to these people in person. What if each day you called six people whom you hadn't talked to for a while? Just call them to chat, not to ask them to buy anything. During the conversation, your business comes up, and you suggest that they stop by to visit when they're in the area. What if they mentioned you to their friends, and your walk-in traffic increased by 20%? Wow.

One great way to expand your "Who knows you" circle is to prepare a short talk on music and senior citizens, or the history of a particular instrument, or the effect music has on raising a child. Offer this talk for free to any service or community group that has regular programs, and your personal visibility and company image will increase threefold.

There's only one hitch. You've got to want to do it. Most people don't. Promoting yourself so that you'll have customers next week means you've got to do something this week. It means a little work. It means half a dozen new phone contacts each day, as many notes or letters, and some after-hour networking. That's what expands your circle of influence from "who do you know?" to a center of influence of people who know you. And the more people who know you (and what you do for a living), the more people who will look to you for a musical instrument when the need arises.

Personal Promotions: When More Business *Really* Matters

You might think that more business is important to anyone who sells for a living. Usually, but not always. There are those business people who use the approach, "What I have is just enough, I don't need more … it doesn't really matter." This group could include salespeople, clerks, or business owners. I hope it's not you, and I hope it's not anyone in your store.

I went looking for an over-the-range microwave oven a few days ago. I had a good idea of what I wanted, and it came down to price, service, and immediate availability. As with most customers, I wanted to be able to talk one-on-one with a salesperson, so I could learn about features and benefits, and make comparisons with other makes and models. I also didn't want to feel like I was paying too much. It had to be from someplace I felt was reliable—if I had a problem, I wanted to know it would be fixed quickly. I didn't want to wait two weeks to get it in my house, I wasn't going to buy it from a catalog, and I wasn't going to order it online. I ended up at Sears.

The salesperson was a young lady named Olga. Olga was definitely not the "pusher" type, but Olga knew the various models inside out. What she didn't know, she brought up on her computer and gave to me in print. I liked Olga. Her English wasn't great, but her tenacity, personality, and direct approach made up for any lack in communication skills.

Like any good customer, I ended up by saying, "I'm going to look around; I'll be back." She replied with, "Hold on, let me check something in my computer. We are having a one-day sale, two days from now. You can save $50. No one else will tell you that, so perhaps you'll come back and ask for me." Well, I came back two days later, asked for Olga, and bought the microwave with all the bells and whistles.

As I left the store I asked for her card, in case I wanted to come back for a new refrigerator. Olga told me she didn't have cards; Sears didn't give her any, and as she put it, "What's the point? Customers either buy or they don't." I took great pride in telling her I had written a book on personal promotion and business cards and would send her a copy. She said "I don't need business cards, I just need to sell the customers who come in."

Olga has her own comfort zone, personal promotion is not important to her. She relies on walk-in traffic. What if Olga really wanted to get her name out there—build up a database of her own? Guess what? It will never happen. That's the difference between selling just enough to make a living and selling a *lot* more than "just enough." This is what separates clerks from salespeople ... the ability to generate business on their own.

Now if you wait or rely on customers to find you on their own, that's okay too. Customers who seek you out are an easy sell. But if more business *really* matters to you, you can do something about it—starting right away. Just concentrate on getting your name out there. Don't rely on your store to create traffic or supply customers. Have people come in to see you *personally*.

Since I wrote *Here's My Card*, salespeople and business people have been sending me their cards and ideas for promoting themselves. The file is starting to overflow. One gentleman wrote asking for a signed copy. I sent him the book, as well as one of my cards. He then wrote back and included his business card. It had a peel-off sticker on the back, so he could adhere it to any surface he wanted. One of his ideas was to stick the card to an envelope as the return address label. This way the recipient had all of his information, and if the envelope sat on a desk, other people would see his card. It's a great idea.

I also received a lot of business cards with titles other than "Sales Manager," or "Assistant VP." Titles like "Head Art Gal," "Director of Interplanetary Sales," and a number of "El Grande Queso" (the big cheese). The idea is to generate some conversation when handing out a card. Get people to like you, and to feel good about spending some money with you.

I think it's great to have the ability to get people to laugh with you. There is a real art to appearing nice and always having a smile on your face, even when you don't feel like it.

One of the better ideas I received was from a lady in New York City. She's a speaker on change and team building, as well as a magician. Her business card is a playing card. When asked for her card, she pulls three playing cards out of her pocket, face up. They are two black cards with a red card in the middle. She then turns them face-down and asks the recipient to pull out the middle card. The diamond or hearts playing card is suddenly her business card! It's terrific. I thought it was so great that I had plenty of sets made, along with instructions. You can be a hit at your next social event—and promote your business at the same time.

An Endless Stream of Customers

I had lunch the other day with a friend of mine who sells pianos. He told me that business for him was starting to get a little soft. Customers aren't coming through the door like they used to. I asked him why. He said he had it figured to a lot of things:

1) The economy is starting to soften.
2) People are waiting to see how things shake out with the new president.
3) The car business is way off and there is a saying, "How GM goes, so goes the nation."
4) The dot.com free fall cost a lot of people a ton of money.
5) His company has a new sales manager and he doesn't know what he's doing.
6) The banks and finance companies are starting to tighten up their credit policies.
7) People are worried about a possible recession.
8) Families are saving for a vacation … like Disneyland or a cruise.
9) The competition is killing them.
10) People only shop price today. Customer service is a thing of the past.

Wow. If "excuses" was an Olympic event, this guy could be a gold medal contender. I asked him exactly what was he doing to try to turn things around. He said he was out of ideas. So then I asked him if he thought about asking for, or following up on, past referrals. He said he didn't like to ask for referrals, doesn't want "bird dogs," and doesn't want to impose on people.

And therein lies the problem. He "doesn't want to."

Referrals are a great source of new customers, but it can't work if you don't ask. The problem is we don't think about it when writing up a sale. The first thing we usually think about is how much we're making on the sale. Then we worry about whether the check is going to clear or if the contract is going to go through. We don't remember to say, "By the way, we get a lot of new business due to referrals from others like yourself who are very excited to be new piano owners. Who do you know who also might be in the market for a quality instrument like this?"

Asking for a referral is step one. You have to ask, and you have to use a little personality at the same time. Believe it or not, most of the time you will get a name. Sometimes two. Then just let it go. Don't start with, "I'll give you a check if they buy," or "If it leads to a sale, I'll give you a commission." That puts them in an awkward position. Friends help out their friends. If you have made them a friend, it's easy to ask for the name of a referral.

Step two is a little different. You have to follow up the referral. That's tougher. It's almost like a cold call. But if you really want more business, you simply *have* to do it. Just pick up the phone and call. If you get an answering machine, just leave your name, phone number, and a message that you've got "good news" for them. Nothing more. People love good news. They will probably return your call.

When you finally get a chance to speak to them (either by you calling them, or when they call you back), explain to them that you got their name from the customer who referred them. Explain you are just doing your job. It's how you earn your living. Be nice. Joke with them. Get them to be your friend on the phone. Don't try to sell them anything. Just try to get an appointment for them to come in to meet you personally. You could tell them that you would like their opinion on a new product that just arrived. Offer them something of perceived value for stopping in. (Lottery tickets, coffee mugs, or T-shirts work great.)

There's a very good chance that if they have even the remotest amount of interest they'll come in to see you. If they don't, and you have established some rapport with them over the phone, ask them if they know somebody who would be interested in what you sell. Tell them again that you're just doing your job. It's how you make a living, and you appreciate anything they can do to help. Again, niceness pays off.

Asking for referrals takes a little bit of a skill—you have to ask at the right time. Ask when they are the most excited, after they sign the contract, when they realize they are finally the owner of your product and can't wait to use it. A day later will be too late. Do it before they leave your place of business.

If they say that they don't know anybody, don't belabor it. You tried. Let them think about it. They might even call you back in a day or two with a name. Or a month later they could mention your name in conversation with someone, remembering that you asked for referrals, and suggest coming in to see you. It just takes that first step of letting them know that referrals are an important part of your business. They could provide you with an endless stream of customers, and those slow periods will pick up faster than you think.

Getting Your Name Out There

Advertising is expensive. Radio drive-time rates are at an all time high—plus, there are more than 25 radio stations in a metro market. Television is no bargain, either. Between cable and satellite services, there are 100 or more channels to choose from—it's tough to know where to spend your money. And then there's the newspaper; circulation is down, and rates are up. What's that tell you? All of a sudden you need a big checkbook and an even bigger crystal ball.

Granted, you have to advertise, but getting your name out there can be done for very little or no cost if you put your PR brain to work. Get some free press, get yourself in the news and create some buzz about your store. You can do it—it just takes a little creative energy.

What have you done—be it an accomplishment, an honor, a donation, or a sponsorship—that could either be a news story for the papers, get you on a talk show, or create a story for a magazine? Let's take a specific example. Won any good awards lately? You might not be nominated for an Emmy, Oscar, Grammy, or Tony, but you may have received something from your local Chamber of Commerce or one of your manufacturers, which could be developed into a news story and get you some print space.

Many business organizations give out annual awards in a variety of categories. Nominate yourself, or have a friend nominate you, for any and every award that you're eligible for. Then send out a press release announcing your nomination. If you become a finalist or a winner, send out additional press releases. With this strategy you can get multiple exposures from a single effort—not to mention the publicity you may get from the sponsoring organization. You also receive the side benefit of being portrayed in an inherently positive light.

What about having your own award ceremony—kind of like Hollywood? Create an employee of the month award, or an employee of the year award. Always do something to honor your employees. Maybe it's someone who has been with you 10, 15, or 25 years. That's news. After all, you wouldn't have been in business one *day* without these employees, never mind years and years. Special plaques and awards are always rewarding and heartwarming. (You can find them by looking under "Advertising Specialties" in the Yellow Pages.) When you give the awards, contact your local media. They may even send a reporter with a camera if it is presented at a dinner, or in front of a large group of people.

And be sure to honor the founders of your company, especially if they are retired from the business. How about having a specific award made up to give to outstanding members of your community? Make it something you design yourself—the more creative, the better. If you're Robert's Guitars, maybe you could have the "Robbie." When someone does something heroic, or something that benefits the whole community, you could give them a "Robbie." Give the award at a special presentation, with a few dignitaries around. Everybody (particularly politicians) likes to see their picture and name in the paper. The more high-visibility people who attend, the better your chance of getting media recognition. In any case, whether you are receiving or presenting an award, your name will be associated with something positive. Prospects will think of your company as one that truly cares about people.

Milestones in your business can make news and get you great PR. For the grand anniversary years—the 25th, 50th and 100th—plan well in advance for maximum media coverage and in-house festivities or banquets. When a business has been successful for 25 years or longer, it should be acknowledged throughout the community. Contact your Chamber of Commerce or mayor's office and see if representatives from these organizations can attend your meetings or banquets. This makes news. A picture of you with your State Assemblyman or Governor could definitely get you in the paper or on TV. Give it a try.

You can also make your own news. That doesn't mean running naked down Main Street and getting arrested. This means doing something that has local interest or community significance that people would like to know about. That's good PR. Local newspapers, local news shows, and local magazines love this type of story. The more interesting you make it, the better your chance of getting coverage.

The main secret to getting free PR is to do it regularly—often, even. How about every couple of weeks or so? You're not going to hit on everything, but getting your name out their with regularity as a news or human interest story can pay big dividends. All it takes is a little effort—but *not* necessarily a lot of cash. Before you know it, your business will be a household name!

Are Your Business Cards Creating More Business for You?

How do you use your business cards? Think about it. How are you putting to use those little billboards you carry in your pocket or purse? Do they sit idly in your desk drawer, only to be tossed out when your area code changes? Or do they come out of your pocket as soon as your customer says, "I'm going to think about it"? Are they great for picking your teeth or writing notes to yourself on the back? Or do they help you create more business or bring customers back one more time?

Check your business cards. Are they current? Do they have all the up-to-date information on how to reach you? Do your cards have your fax number, your cell phone number, your e-mail address? Do they have information about your website? Are they a good representation of your business and yourself? When you give out a card, does it look brand new, or does it look like it's been used once or twice before?

An e-mail address on a business card shows that you're keeping up with the times. Listing fax and cell phone numbers shows that you're very accessible. And a card that isn't stained or dog-eared shows that you are concerned with quality and appearance. But that's just the beginning. How you put them to use is just as important as the look of the cards themselves. Some businesspeople take their cards to another level. There's a kitchen and bath dealer in Idaho whose business card has a fold-over with a perforated edge that becomes a discount coupon. It's used as an incentive for coming into the store.

How about the back of your business cards? Is this space used at all? Several companies use the reverse side of their cards to print a map and directions to the business. One business owner uses the back of his card for his web page address and e-mail address, plus a small version of his home page.

With the amount of phone numbers and other information you might want to list on your business card, don't make the mistake of trying to cram it all onto one side. That's why the fold-over card with three to four sides of usable space is an option. One rule of thumb is to make sure that you can put a quarter somewhere on your business card without covering any type. If there isn't enough blank space to set a quarter on it somewhere, you may be overdoing it. So before you put your company slogan, the number of years you've been in business, five phone, fax, and cellular numbers, and the names of all of the lines you carry on one side of your business card, think about your company image, the possibility of confusing the customer, and whether your business card will stand out from your competition's.

Something else. You can have different cards for different uses. Maybe you want a card with a coupon for outside events. Or you may have a special card to leave with a tip in a restaurant on which you can write "bring this in for a free gift."

This does not mean that you have to spend thousands of dollars on business cards. Some of the most creative forms require little or no money. In fact, one bike dealer in New Jersey seldom gives out his regular card. When a customer tells him she's "going to think about it" and asks for his card, he says he doesn't "have one at his fingertips." Then he goes to his

desk, pulls out his checkbook and rips a check in half so just the store name, address and phone number is on it. He writes his name on the bottom and says, "use this." It really gets a customer's attention.

A friend of mine says that he doesn't like to have business cards that are the same shape and size as all of his competitors', so when a customer asks for his card, he merely goes to his desk, takes out an index card and writes his name, address, and phone number on it. He says that it really stands out from the little stack of regular business cards the customer has been accumulating from other people in his business. It's certainly a lot bigger, doesn't get lost, and has a personal touch. And when he writes, "I want to earn your business!" in longhand, it really means something.

If you're using your business cards in a way that makes it easy for customers to leave your business, you might want to rethink the whole process. And if your business card is out of date or very ordinary, you might want to take a long look at what it would take to make it a good reflection of yourself.

Business cards can bring business in, they can bring customers back, and they can be one of the best methods of personal advertising you have. Take a look at some of the business cards you have collected yourself. If your business card doesn't match their uniqueness and go beyond their creativity, now's the time to do something about it.

Simple Steps to Simpler Promotions

Getting your name out there to create more customers is what the retail business is all about. People have to know about you, what you do or sell, and where you are. You want to look like you are not only in business, but you are successful at it as well. Only problem is, sometimes it takes a crystal ball to forecast what's going to work, and other times it takes a big checkbook. Promoting yourself and your business is kind of a "what" thing rather than a "why" science. We find out what works and what doesn't. We just don't know why.

Promoting your store can be expensive if you're running newspaper ads, TV spots, and commercials on drive-time radio. Usually, only half of it is ever effective. The trouble is, we just don't know which half. And what do you do if you don't have a checkbook that can take that kind of hit? Do you just cut back or give up altogether?

As a new businessman, I too faced these questions and dilemmas. I remember just starting out in retail years ago. I started with a small store, a small inventory, and little cash. I bought a van that I also used as my personal vehicle. It was nicely lettered with my company's name on each side. I wanted my business to look big, and to look like I was already successful. On the back I had lettered "Mobile unit #6." The left side was lettered "Mobile Unit #5," and the other side had "Mobile Unit #7." It looked like a different truck coming and going. Customers would come in a say, "I see your trucks all over the place." I loved it, and it worked.

For a while we didn't even have business cards. When someone would ask us for a card, we'd just grab an invoice, and explain that all of our identification information was already on those. The salesperson would write their name on the top of the invoice, and whichever model they were looking at, along with the price. It was almost like writing up a deal, and it was more effective and memorable than handing out a card.

Each holiday season, the newspaper in our town expanded as stores geared up for shoppers. My competitors pulled out all the stops with huge ads. I couldn't compete. Instead, I scattered 14 one-inch by one-inch ads, with a sale item, special product, or discount coupon throughout the paper. Customers would come in and say, "I saw your ad on every page." Perception was the key. Success breeds success, and I knew if I looked successful I was going to be successful.

I'm a big believer in portable, lighted road signs. You can rent them at any equipment rental place. For preferred customer nights I would have the sign read, "THIS IS THE SALE YOU HEARD ABOUT ON TV!" Then I'd paper the windows with sale signs, bring in balloons, and send out a few hundred direct-mail pieces. I'd also run a couple of classified crawl ads on the local cable station. I would have point of sale cards about a special three-day sale, coffee and donuts, a plate of cheese, and a couple of bottles of inexpensive wine—all for less than $300.

Another unique promotional idea involved copying a few hundred sale fliers. I'd take the fliers and crumple them up and then flatten them out. Then I'd fold them into thirds, and stick them in an envelope with a handwritten note that read, "This is too important to throw away. Here it is again." The fliers would be sent to groups of people who were possibly in the market for our product. Can you imagine the person opening the envelope? I guess the old saying, "First you get money, then you get integrity," is somewhat true. It was just another fun way I found to promote my store on a limited budget.

I learned that sometimes you just have to think on your feet, and take advantage of any situation that might bring more people through your door. You can't worry about not having enough bucks to spend. Creative promotion on a limited budget can be simple if you just think about what you want to derive from it. Get some input from the rest of the people in your organization. There are no bad ideas. Where's your next simple promotion coming from?

Using Celebrities at Your Next Promotion

Celebrities at your store bring in traffic, and they can turn a slow weekend into a blockbuster event if you do it the right way. It doesn't have to be a major rock star, movie star, or sports celebrity either. (Of course that would be a plus). It could be something as simple as your local weatherman, a native hometown major-league ballplayer, or any type of local hero. You want somebody who will attract people out of curiosity, controversy, nostalgia, or admiration. And you also want somebody who will help you sell. It would be great to have The Rolling Stones, or just Mick himself, but if you shell out mega-bucks, and sell nothing, you haven't accomplished a whole lot.

I loved this article in *Automotive News*: "Having a slow sales month? With the Sopranos on your side, you can make a killing." It seems that for the price of $5,000 to $10,000 per actor, a minimum of three cast members from the HBO show *The Sopranos* will appear at a dealership for a few hours or more, sign autographs, and attract a lot of people. The show's leading actors James Gandolfini and Edie Falco aren't for dealership rent, but you can get "Ralphie (Joe Pantoliano), "Furio" (Federico Castelluccio), "Bobbie Bacala" (Steve R. Schrripa), and others.

They are booked doing these events for the next two months. One dealer who brought them in sold more than 100 cars by letting the buyers take a test drive with the star. Another dealer charged $35 per person and donated the money to charity. Each visitor received an autographed picture, food, drinks, and a free car wash, while taking a look at the latest models of new cars. About 5,000 people showed up, and 187 cars went out the door. That degree of celebrity promotion might be a little too much for smaller businesses, but you can scale it down and do it on a smaller budget with great success.

Years ago I did a couple of promotions with Mickey Mantle and Clayton Moore (The Lone Ranger). They were strictly retail events to move merchandise. It wasn't just to see how many people would come to the store. I found it takes a little planning and forethought to get a celebrity promotion to work.

The key to making a celebrity promotion a success is to involve the celebrity in the sale, even if they share only a few words with the customer. Hanging around and handing out signed pictures is not going to turn merchandise. Having them suggest to a customer that they buy, will. When we held a promotion called "It's a Brand New Ballgame" at our store, Mickey Mantle talked to everyone. He was genuinely a good guy, but he didn't really want to know anything about our business. So, when I told a customer that we would have to check with Mickey about a price concession, I would make sure to go over to him and end my question with "What do you think Mickey?" And Mickey would always answer, "OK with me, but they've got to buy it today." And then he would go back to shaking hands and signing baseballs. He was a part of the store.

The Lone Ranger was equally as good. Clayton Moore really thought he was The Lone Ranger— he never even took his mask off. And when he talked, you knew the voice. He was believable. If he said, "We'd appreciate your business here today," you bought. You could have your picture taken with him afterward—signing on the dotted line came first.

Bringing in celebrities to help generate store traffic can be a great idea, if it's not overdone, not over budget, and if you have a goal in mind. It's great to be a hero to your community, but you want to be a hero to your accountant and banker as well. A crowd too big could trash your store, pilfer merchandise, and wreak havoc. Maybe you have a friend who has made the news, or has become a sports or media celebrity. They might come in for a favor, or for a small fee. Perhaps someone who was a legend in yesteryear would love the chance to make an appearance at your store for a nominal fee. Remember, it depends on the audience you're trying to reach and who you want in your store. If you cater to younger people, a star from *The Lawrence Welk Show* won't make it. And older people won't come to meet a MTV celebrity and they probably won't care too much about a skateboard champion. It depends on what you want to promote, how much you want to spend, and what you expect to achieve.

An afternoon with a celebrity in your store can do wonders for a slow business period, and it can get people talking about you for a long time afterwards. You may even get free publicity from your local papers and TV and radio stations might want an interview. Your store's name could have celebrity status, even if it's only for a few hours. But remember, you still want to sell. Sales have to exceed cost. You are in business to turn a profit. Using a celebrity for a promotion can help bring customers in. Make sure that person can also help you sell as well.

Does Your Music Store Have a Newsletter?

I am amazed at the number of small music dealers that send out a monthly newsletter on upcoming events, sale items, playing tips, concert schedules, lesson programs, and so on. You might not think of it as a big thing, but I think it's pretty cool.

I'm not talking about e-mail newsletters, but honest-to-goodness, hold-in-your-hand print pieces that are sent through the mail. Not e-zines, but actual paper pieces. Maybe e-mail newsletters will replace paper communications someday, but no matter what you think, for now, paper is very much alive, as is evident by what you are holding in your hand and reading right now.

A free newsletter is a good paper weapon for music stores competing with other local dealers, the Internet, discount catalogues, mass-market retailers, and big-box store competition. It establishes you as an authority in your business, and it keeps your name in front of your customers.

Plus, you can use your newsletter as a mailer or handout promotional piece. Another great thing about a store newsletter is that it is a subtle and inoffensive way to remind indifferent prospects about you and why you are better than other music stores in your area. It could even make you look bigger than you really are, if that's what you want. Some music dealers put a price on the newsletter to give it perceived value, even though it is sent at no cost.

The whole idea behind a store newsletter is to make money for you. You can easily weave your instruments and services into the stories, and tie events and developments in your music biz articles. However, you don't want to be too obvious or heavy-handed, since most people won't read (or save) something they construe as a puff-piece or just sales material. They will read and save something that contains useful information. It's up to you to create that worthiness.

A successful newsletter can be as simple as one-sheet prepared on your computer, or as sophisticated as four to eight pages written and printed professionally, with pictures, charts, and graphics. Newsletters should be distributed monthly (and certainly not less than quarterly). Anything less is too infrequent to have meaningful impact.

You can get the input of your staff for articles, stories, and ideas each month. These articles are a great way to offer added-value for your customers. Get local music teachers to come up with playing hints, manufacturers to supply new product information, and use snippets from industry news that your customers might value reading. You might want to highlight some of your customers once in awhile to add to your local interest.

Bob Carbone of Music Melody Manor in Clay, New York, hides names of customers throughout his monthly newsletter. If your name appears in the publication, you are entitled to a special gift for coming in, plus a discount certificate on a future purchase. Other dealers offer a printed coupon, preferred customer savings, and limited specials in the newsletter. They're not writing blatant advertising, but tying advertising in with informational material. This is a great guerilla marketing approach that your competition won't usually be aware of (at least not right away) and a good way to increase floor traffic. The key is to offer fresh, useful, and interesting content.

If your salespeople need a way to keep in touch with past customers, search out new ones, and keep people coming through the door, a store newsletter could be a big help. They could send out a few each day to their own circle of influence, then call the people to see if they got it and call attention to something in the print piece they might be interested in.

I think it's important that all music store salespeople have a game plan to bring customers in on their own. Think of how much more business you could do with eight or 10 extra customers a day! Granted, this is no big deal if you are a 20,000-square-foot store with a six-figure advertising budget, but for small to medium size stores, 52 weeks of that many more customers adds significantly to the bottom line.

CHAPTER 7:
Selling

The Shortest Distance Between Two Points

I was never very good at math in high school. I remember failing geometry and having to take it again in order to graduate. It was a real pain, but 40+ years later I can still tell you that the three methods of proving congruent triangles are angle-side-angle, side-angle-side, and side-side-side, and that the shortest distance between two points is a straight line. The triangle thing never got me very far, but the straight line philosophy comes into play quite often—particularly in sales and marketing. It's an effective one-on-one approach to increasing business.

There are tons of books on finding customers and closing sales, but many of the ideas could be condensed into one basic straight line approach booklet on just simply "asking." "Asking" is a straight line method—asking prospects and customers to buy, asking for referrals, asking people to come into your store, and asking what it would take to get them to do more business with you.

Years ago a man by the name of Judge Ziglar (brother of sales guru, Zig Ziglar) wrote a book called *Timid Salesmen Have Skinny Kids*. It was a book on basic assertiveness—things like asking for the order, asking for repeat business, and asking for someone's help in increasing sales. One of today's problems, though, is that even though we know what could improve business, we sometimes go out of our way not to do it. We don't take the shortest distance between two points.

For example, there's a Volkswagen dealership in our town whose sales have been soft recently. They blame the current economy, explaining that people are hanging on to their cars longer until things get better. But I know for a fact that two of my female friends have gone in there to look at either the new Beetle or the new Jetta ... and left without anyone talking to them. They knew what they were looking for, and had every intention of buying upon finding a car they liked. But since they were by themselves, apparently the salesmen didn't think they were viable prospects. No one asked them any questions. No one approached them. One lady ended up buying a Honda Accord, and the other bought from another VW dealer. A little assertiveness would have done wonders for the guys, who never came out of their offices.

Think about it, how many times have you gone into a store as a customer and nobody talked to you? I bet it's a lot. Some salespeople/clerks just don't want to bother. They let customers look, and if they want to buy something, they have to bring it to the counter or find a salesperson to interrupt. It happens every day. Simple sales strategy starts with opening your mouth and talking to the customer.

My neighbor's daughter is 14 years old, and saved up some money to buy a guitar. She wanted to make her own decision, and went out looking by herself. She went to three music stores before somebody took the time to explain some features and benefits to her and take her money. She told me one store's salespeople treated her like an intrusion on their day, and she won't spend her money with anyone who was rude to her. But the salesperson at the store that got her business simply said to her, "We'd like you as a customer for years to come. Here's a guitar that should be just what you're looking for. Would you like to get it?" She said, "They didn't tell me to bring back my parents, or to put the guitar down until someone comes over to demonstrate it." They were nice to her, didn't treat her like a child, and asked her to buy—a straight-line approach. She tells all her friends where she got the guitar. That's kidfluence in action. Recognizing that kids have money, and can make decisions too, is the shortest distance between two points—your product and the cash register.

Here's a great success story on straight-line marketing. There's a men's clothing store between my office and the garage where I park my car. I pass it every day. It's been open for about three months; they advertise in the local papers, change their displays every month, and have weekend sales, one-day sales, and inventory clearance sales. They advertise "mall selections at discount prices." I have never gone into the store. Last week I was on my way to the garage when the store manager was coming out the door. We made eye contact, I nodded hello and she said to me, "I see you go by every day, why don't you ever come in here to look around?" I didn't have a good answer, and since I had a few minutes, I walked in. She said, "Take a look at these new shirts, and here's a line of pants that would go great with them." In 15 minutes I spent $200, and was happy. I've been back again since, but I would still be passing by if she hadn't asked. And asking in selling it the shortest distance between a customer and a sale.

If your sales need a little shot in the arm, maybe it's time to take a more direct approach. When a customer leaves without buying, ask them why. If you meet people who have never been to your store, ask why. You might not like all the answers, but it could be a real learning experience, and it could also increase your numbers by the end of the month.

Getting Right to the Point

My granddaughter Emily called me the other day. She and her mom are coming up from Memphis to visit for a week. She wanted to make sure I had some things to eat that she would like, and said if I was going to the grocery store that I should pick up some apple juice, Pop Tarts, and Cocoa Pebbles. She informed me that, if she thought of anything else, she would e-mail the list to me. My granddaughter is seven. I told her that if she e-mailed me, I would e-mail her back to let her know I got the updated list of groceries. Emily said, "If you e-mail me back, don't make it really long, otherwise call me." I thought about that for awhile. Here is a seven-year-old child asking for simplified communication. Is there something here?

Billboards are rarely effective if they are more than seven words. TV commercials with too much information are not advisable, and rapid-fire, fast-talking, too much hype radio spots don't make it either.

Mark Twain once told the story about listening to a preacher in church. The preacher was highly motivating, a great storyteller, and very inspirational. He was so good at preaching that Mark Twain thought about putting $10 in the collection basket when it came around. The preacher kept going on and on, and Twain thought maybe $5 would be enough. The preacher rambled and Twain thought $2 would be ample. When the collection basket was passed, and half the congregation was nodding off, he thought about *taking* a dollar. Simple speaking can have great rewards. When it becomes long, complicated, and overdone, it can have the opposite effect.

We live in an age of over-communication. Be competitive—get right to the point. And do it in words that everyone can understand. Talk in terms a 12-year-old can understand. Use one and two syllable words. Being clever at the same time isn't bad, either. Ever notice that when you thumb through a magazine quickly, and there's a cartoon on a certain page, you always go back and read it? You know it's quick, easy-to-read, and might make you smile. You might skip the lengthy stories and articles, but you always glance at the cartoons.

Most people try to avoid the panhandlers at metro train stations. I was in Manhattan's Penn Station recently; a lot of people looking for handouts had signs. Some you couldn't help but notice, like the one that read, "Residentially Challenged." The best one I saw said, "My wife's been kidnapped, and I am a dollar short of the ransom." These people got attention. And they got money too.

In selling, if we start rambling without getting a customer's attention first, those people start looking at other things to focus on. Getting to the point quickly can make the difference. It's amazing how even simple point-of-sale signs can be effective. For years I have joked that if you're doing an outside exposure promotion, put a small sign on your main product that reads "Now Legal In (your state)." People will line up to ask why the sign was there. They'll search out someone to ask if it was illegal before. When you tell them you were just trying to get someone's attention to ask about the product, all of a sudden you're in a conversation—and that's where it all starts. From there it's just a matter of quickly getting to the point.

I'll give you an example of short, clever, and to the point. Somewhere in your store (on an item you would like customers to ask about), place or attach a small sign that says "Don't Ask." See how many people ask about it. Human nature is something else. If you took the same item and listed 15 features and benefits, along with price, discount, and savings, you wouldn't get half the interest.

One of the biggest mistakes salespeople make is overselling the product. That goes for the company whose advertising and marketing strategies sometimes go off on tangents as well. For the salesperson, just find a need and fill it. With advertising, show how a need can be filled. And be quick about it. It can be that simple.

Getting right to the point can free up a lot of time for you when talking to a customer. When you get the first sign of positive acceptance, you could ask, "Would you like to get it?" If the customer says "yes," you could easily save yourself an hour of sales-babble. I liked a sign I saw in a music store the other day. "This instrument can take your career to another level—$1,850 takes it home." Right to the point.

The late Robert Sandler used to say, "Take a customer's buying temperature at least once during a presentation." His trick for getting right to the point was, "On a scale of 1 to 10; 1 being you hate it and can't stand it, and 10 being you can't wait to get it in your home, where do we stand right now?" Then, whatever the answer, he would always say, "What do I have to do to get it to a 10?" Very direct. It saves a lot of time.

We're in an age of complicated communication—over-wrought with high technology and bombarded with thousands of sales and marketing messages a day. Make it easy for your prospect. Make it simple for your customer. Just get right to the point.

The Human Side of Selling

I was flying from Pittsburgh to Grand Rapids a week or so ago. The flight attendant began with the usual safety instructions. And as usual, not a whole lot of passengers were paying attention. My nose was buried in the second section of *USA Today*. Other people were looking out the window, shutting off cellular phones, or closing their eyes. Suddenly I heard her say "For those of you who haven't been in a car since 1957, here's how the seat belt works." I looked up, and so did some other passengers. It was a real person talking without a script. Then she said, "Listen to the next part about the oxygen mask, because there will be a quiz." Now everybody was listening. It was a human being with actual expression and emotion, not a robotic, automated speech we were hearing. This wasn't Southwest Airlines where they kid around as a general rule. This was US Airways, where flight attendants are more worried about losing their job, than winning happy passengers. The human touch can do wonders.

How often do we talk about the same products, same features and benefits, and use the same spiel day in and day out? It gets to be so repetitive that you feel like you can open your mouth and the words will come out automatically.

Do you use the phrases "Thanks for coming in," "Have a nice day," "Here's my card," or "Can I help you?" with no inflection or interest? Do you answer the phone by saying your company's name and let the words all run together in an unclear and monotone voice? Yesterday I called a car service center and heard "This is Monroe. We fix mufflers and service air conditioners. These damn phones are ringing off the hook can I help ya?" I hung up. They are not touching any of my cars.

I had a better experience a few days later when I went into a boat dealership and was met with a big smile and the words, "Hi, you've come to the right place if you want to put a lot of fun in your life. Do you have a boat now?" I like it when a salesperson makes me feel like I'm her most important customer at the moment. I don't like to feel like I'm an intrusion on someone's day.

How about you? Does your personality come through when you talk to a customer? People will speak with and respect those they consider a peer. The more natural you sound, the easier it will be to put a sale together. We tune out, and are often annoyed by unemotional, canned sales pitches. Pitches like the ones you hear when you pick up the phone (after saying hello several times) and a monotone voice greets you with, "Hello, can I speak to (insert bad mispronunciation of your name)?" Then they begin reading a script.

Of course you want to be prepared when you describe your products and services. The worst time to be thinking about what you will say is when it is about to leave your mouth. For example, think about the bad acting you've seen in plays or movies. It sounded stilted, and unnatural—like it was being read. When you talk to a customer, you want to come across to them like they are talking to a friend, not a machine.

Think about this. Are you putting together ads and direct mail pieces that are bland, boring, and trigger no response because they're the same old, same-old? I had a vacancy in one of my rental units last month. One of my friends owns a couple of units there as well, and he was telling me his classified ads don't get a lot of response. His ads list the generic: two bedroom, one-and-a-half baths, with washer and dryer hookup, garage, basement, and deck. Security required. Now, believe it or not, the people in the classified department of our local paper told him to do it this way. Use abbreviations, limited letters, save money. Don't spend cash on needless words. I was worried that I wouldn't get a lot of calls, so I decided to put it in terms people could relate to. My ad read "Very lovely 2 br. apt with 1.5 baths, on quiet street with park-like setting. Don't miss this opportunity." I listed my home phone and cellular phone prefaced by the words "I am very reachable." The clerk taking the ad was shocked. She said, "You don't need all those words. You are paying four times too much." I ran the ad. I received 84 calls.

There is a mailing company in Southern California that will supply you with any list you want, and then mail your direct mail piece. They attach a yellow Post-It note with the handwritten words "Get this. It's Great!" It is signed " J." They have been doing this for years. You would think people would have figured it out by now. But it's the human touch that works. I guess it doesn't get old. Maybe you've thrown away a dozen of these by now, but I bet you always check first to see if it came from one of your friends. The added creativity gets you 10 times the response. The personal touch makes it happen.

If customers want to deal with a cold, impersonal source, they'll go to the Internet or a catalog. You are at an advantage because you can use personality, inflection, kindness, understanding, and warmth when you meet a customer. You can make a customer a friend, get them to smile, and have them refer you to their friends. Take advantage of it.

It doesn't matter if you're selling flutes, pianos, guitars, or drums. It could be pro audio, lighting, or keyboards. Let your human touch show through. Tweak your personality. Find out what kind of music your customer likes to play or listen to. Get them to laugh a little. Don't treat them like it's an effort to take their money. The music business is a fun business. The more instruments you sell, the more fun it can be.

Reading Your Customer's Mind

It would be great if we had the power to know what goes on inside our customers' heads when we show them a new guitar, set of drums, or state-of-the-art digital piano. When you ask them if they'd like to buy it, do they say, "I want to think it over"? What are they really thinking? Does that "think it over," mean "I want to check a couple discount catalogs," or "I want to go back and buy it from the music store I just came from?" And when you say to your customer, "Would you pay cash, or would you like to finance this?" wouldn't it be great to know in advance what the answer would be? OK. Maybe we don't have the power to read customers' minds, and maybe we can't predict the future, but we can *anticipate* what the outcome will be. We can ask customers questions where we already know in advance what the answers will be. We can lead them where we want them to go. This can take our sales skills up a notch or two right away.

You can call this anticipatory closing, predictable qualifying, or any number of fancy terms. Actually it's more like common sense selling. Hockey great Wayne Gretzky once said his secret was that he skated to where the puck was going to be, no matter where it was. The "Black Widow" pool wizard Jeanette Lee always knows where her fourth, fifth, and sixth shots are going to be after the break. If you already know the answers to questions you're going to ask, you're more likely to make more sales. It's like the shoe salesman asking the customer, "What do you think—would you like to take these with you, or would you like to wear them?" You anticipate a positive response. "No, I don't want them," is not an option.

If you're selling a piano and the issue is price, what if you asked, "Do you want a bench that holds music?" Most people do. Most benches have a lift top lid. You anticipate a "yes" and the more positive responses you get out of a customer, the closer you are to a sale.

If you're selling a guitar, and you ask, "Are you going to want extra strings?" and then you ask, "How many sets would you like?" you are way past the point of asking for the guitar sale. You anticipated the sale. Now it's just a matter of add-ons.

If you're selling an electronic keyboard for the home, and during the demo you ask, "Would you play this if you had it in your home?" you know what the answer will be. Don't go for a "no" go for a "yes." Anticipatory selling. It can work.

When a customer comes in to buy an accessory item, and asks if you have a certain type of drumstick, a particular set of guitar strings, or a certain model of microphone, instead of saying, "yes," try saying, "Certainly, how many would you like?" Anticipate that they'll want more than one. And while they're thinking about your question, you can say "I can get you (a dozen) (a case) (six or more) if you want." You anticipate that they will need more than they came in for, and you might get what you anticipate.

How about this? When customers come look-ing for an expensive instrument and tell you in advance that this is the first place they've looked, anticipate that this is going to be their major objection for not buying then and there. So you can say things like, "Am I showing this to you so you can look around?" Or "Are you just checking prices to see if you can do better someplace else?" Anticipate their objection and head it off at the pass. You can say things like, "Obviously you're a pro at this; you're probably wondering why this is so cheap, aren't you?" Or throw in "We don't have a lot of these, so you  might want to make a quick decision before they're gone." "It's a hot item and the price is right." And if it applies, you could say, "Would you like to use this on your gig tonight? I can make it happen for you." Anticipate that they're revved up about the ax, want to use it right away, and don't want to look like a weenie in your eyes. You sell to the best musicians, don't you? Make your prospects think they want to be included in that group. Anticipate what questions will play to their egos.

Sometimes you want to anticipate that you're going to get beaten up over price. Don't let customer knowledge of discount prices from other dealers take you by surprise. Anticipate that customers have this in their brains before they open their mouths. Sell yourself, your store, and the instru-ment all at the same time. And when you say, "Hey, didn't you open for Billy Joel," and you know the answer is "no," anticipate that at least you have their attention and they'll know you think that they're the best play-ers who ever came in the store. They are. They're your customers. Play to your audience.

Suggestive Selling

I had an interesting conversation last week with an order taker from Heartland America. Actually the call was a learning experience. Heartland America is a catalog company that deals with closeouts, overstocked, discounted, and reconditioned items. If an informercial doesn't do well, the too-good-to-be-true item ends up in the catalog.

I called to order a set of Adams golf wedges that were $200 off the retail price, plus I had a $20 discount coupon, and was entitled to free shipping. After a series of telephone prompts, a woman answered and asked how she could help me. I started by giving her the account code on the back of the catalog, but she said "Wait, wait … tell me what you want to order first, so in case it isn't available you won't waste a lot of time." That sounded like great customer service, so I told her the item number of the golf clubs, and she said they were in stock. She also said, "That's not one of the items everybody calls about." So I asked her, "What items do a lot of people call about?" She said "One of them is the AT&T cordless phone with digital answering machine. They are normally priced at $114, but they're in the catalog for $39, less 10% off. There are only a few left. Do you want one?" I thought about this for a minute. Everybody is ordering them and there are only a few left. Of course, put me down for one, I told her. So then I asked her what else was everybody ordering? She told me about the Panasonic fax/copier of which there were only a very few left in stock. The suggested retail for the machine was $249.95, but the catalog price was $129 with a $20 mail-in rebate, less my 10% discount. She asked me if I would like one and I said, "Sure."

Then she said, "I don't want you to think I'm telling you about these things because I'm on commission. You sound like a sharp person, and I just want you to be aware of some incredible buys." I was hooked. My $99 order turned into $624.50. I asked her if she always handled her phone orders this way. She told me that most callers are quick and to the point, and get annoyed if their item isn't available. She also said that she found that many people don't look through the whole catalog and don't know what else is in there. Besides, many items don't last very long.

She took great pride in telling me the value of getting people to trust you over the phone. She also said people sometimes like to be guided in their purchase and can't make a decision, so you have to help them. She thought that by telling a customer everybody else was buying a product, they would want one too. Also, previous customers know that many items have extremely limited quantities, and time can be of the essence. I told her this was great "suggestive selling," and she had been trained pretty well. She said this was her own idea, and it helped established some rapport with the customers. I thought this was great, and to help her along, I suggested she tell some of the customers that she owned or tried the product as well, to give it some credibility. She said she doesn't get the opportunity to try many items, and she can't afford to buy most of them. She was only 18 and was still in school. Wow! Is that great or what? I thought I was speaking to someone much older. She was just out of high school and had already figured out what it takes to get additional sales, selling products through using her own personality along with some street smarts.

Think about it. Do you try and help customers with their decision to purchase? Do you suggest add-ons, or are you just so happy they bought something that you rush to get their money before they change their mind? If you own the product yourself, do you tell them how happy you are with it? Do you tell customers what the really hot items are that you have in stock and that everyone must have? Do you let them know that some items have limited availability, particularly when everybody is interested? Not only that, how about telling your customers about other people who own the product and are very happy? They could be past customers, well-known people, or even local celebrities. If the mayor of your town, the football coach, or the sports anchor on local TV owns what you sell, tell your customer. They might feel that if those people like it and use it, they would be happy with it as well.

"Suggestive selling" is not R-rated, or X-rated. It is G-rated. It appeals to everybody. Everybody wants some help in making up their mind, and it's up to you to help them. Use your personality and charm, along with some common-sense and a little push, and your sales could increase dramatically.

Are Your Employees Speaking Without Listening?

First of all, I am 100% Ukrainian. I don't know if you know anyone else who is, but I am. I want to share a few things with you about my Ukrainian heritage. My father lived in a little town at the foot of the Carpathian mountains called Kartuziv. My grandparents were from Pydhaychi, about 12 miles away. I am proud that I am Ukrainian. The first words I remember from my mother were (phonetically), "Yah toh be dahm, e detih de domo" which loosely translated means, "Go in the house; you're going to get spanked." The golf balls I play with have "Cool Hand Uke" logo-ized on them, and I subscribe to the *Ukrainian Observer*, a monthly magazine from Ukraine. It was in this magazine that I found out about "language fraud" in the US.

The article said to be on guard for some words and phrases Americans use. It said to be careful of a whole series of clichés that set you up for a proverbial fall. I share some of them with you in the hopes your staff never falls into the trap of using them. The first word the article said to look out for is the word "frankly." Whenever anyone starts off a sentence with "frankly," you can "pretty much be assured they are going to lie to you." Also, be careful of "to be perfectly honest with you ..." That means they are going to lie to you as well. It said "used car salesmen and people selling automatic slicers on TV are most likely to use these words." Also, the word "like" when used as emphasis usually comes from people with lower IQs. You might hear, "Man, like, you must be kidding" or "That is, like, the greatest product on the market." "Like" is used by people with less education, the magazine said. Another phrase to look out for was "with all due respect." Look out. That means that there is no respect intended.

The *Observer* went on to say that the Americans who frequently use the word "awesome" probably don't get out much, and the phrase "ballpark figure" is not of much value, because American ballparks are of all different sizes. The center field fence in Cincinnati's old Riverfront stadium was at 420 feet, but in the team's new stadium, it's 15 feet closer. Their suggestion is "When an American wants to give you a ballpark figure, ask, 'What ballpark?'" I found that very funny.

I thought the last paragraph in the article was the best. It said, "These are tired American expressions that you best tune out. Using these terms in business is about as professional as coming to work without proper clothes or not having bathed in a week."

I could add a bunch more that I find people who work in music stores regularly use. "Hep 'ya?" comes to mind first. I realize that's just a form of "Can I help you?" and it cuts down on the time it takes to get the words out of a salesperson's mouth. Of course, the answer for "hep 'ya?" is usually "just looking." You don't make many sales with those words. The other phrase that seems to be uttered at every cash register is "y'all set?" A customer might come to the counter with a set of guitar strings in hand and the intention of getting information on a digital keyboard or guitar amp. Typically, when a customer finds no one else to talk to, he or she comes to the counter and invariably the cash register/counter person says, "Y'all set?" I have seen this for myself countless times. "Y'all set" translates into, "How fast can I get you out of here?" Sears does it. Department stores do it. At least grocery stores elaborate with, "Did you find everything you were looking for?" Taking a little more time with the customer could result in more sales.

When a customer asks the price of an expensive instrument, the proper response is not, "It's kind of pricey" (I heard that several times this past week). "A lot less than you think" would be a better answer, if the price is not clearly posted. That response could put the customer in a receptive mood, while the price is being checked. Over a heavy selling holiday season, salespeople get barraged with the same basic questions over and over again. All of a sudden the answers come out almost without thinking. Customers ask, "Are there more in stock?" "Do you have one in the box?" or "Do you carry other makes?" and one or two word answers come back, such as "Yep," "Nope," and "Don't know." Customers ask a price, and the salesperson gives a price without saying, "Would you like to get it?" Giving the right answer just takes a little common sense, some street smarts, and the ability to listen to ourselves while we talk. A little attention to what we say could add up to bigger revenue. You could also sell a few more Ukrainians that way as well.

Do You Have Customers Who Fear "Transaction Time"?

When customers walk into your store, they have some fears that even they might not be aware of. And just because they're not aware of them, doesn't mean that the fears don't exist. Those fears and anxieties are hidden back there in your customers' subconscious minds, and sometimes it's good to address them right away, even before they come to the front part of your customers' brains.

The first fear is "the quality of the goods." You only stock the very best musical instruments, and you want to let your customers know that as soon as you give any kind of product demo. That's a pretty easy feat if you believe in the instruments you sell.

The second fear is "if the price is fair." Nobody wants to get ripped off. They don't want to pay too much. The value has to exceed the price. Make sure the value is so high that customers feel you didn't go too deeply into their pockets.

The third fear is "other people's opinions." When they get that new guitar home, have a new grand piano delivered to their living room, or bring the new sound equipment to their next gig, no one wants to hear, "You bought a *what*?" No customers want to be ridiculed about their purchases after they leave the store. To hit this head-on, make sure your customer knows what famous artists play the same equipment, and what other local people (maybe friends or neighbors) also bought the same instrument and are extremely happy with it. Keep a customer/instrument list handy so you can drop a name or two when the time comes. And know what famous groups or musicians use the equipment. A picture on the wall or a name during the demo can do wonders.

The last fear is something that not too many music retailers/salespeople address. It is "fear of invoice" or "fear of transaction time." When customers agonize over a purchase, hear your feature and benefit story, listen to your demo, then realize that they have to drop a serious amount of cash, having to sign their names on the bottom line can be a bit of a trip. This fear can be overcome by simply having an invoice with you (maybe in your pocket), and putting it down somewhere nearby during the demo, so your customer knows that sooner or later, this is where the whole little session is going to end up. It's nothing new. Insurance people have been doing it for years. Every policy has the "sign here" form in view while the policy is being read.

We want to make it easy for the customer to buy. I remember years ago, a piano salesperson spent two hours with a customer, getting a "Yes, we'll take it," and then said, "OK, let's go do the awful paperwork." The customer walked. It was fear of invoice, fear of signing her name, fear of too tedious of a process. Make it a simple easy-to-do buying event.

But transaction time is a factor as well. It's another fear. In today's age of drive-in banks, drive-through restaurants, and drive-up drugstores, no one wants to wait any more. Grocery stores have express lines for six items, 12 items or less, 15 items or less, or they'll open another register if there are more than two people in line. If we buy gas, we want to pay at the pump. And the pump better not be slow, either. Microwave ovens, fast food, convenience stores. We have to compete.

A good friend of mine went into one of the big-box music stores in Florida, looked around, and picked up one of those "shaker eggs." You know, the cool little music accessory item that is fun to play with, and can make you the life of the party after a couple of drinks. He decided to buy a whole box. The closest salesperson to ring it up was, as he puts it, "a hundred yards away." He couldn't get anybody's attention. Nobody came over to talk to him. He finally put it down and left. So much for that sale. No telling what else he would have bought. He said, "Maybe they should put those guys on Rollerblades™. At least I would have had quicker service, and I sure-as-heck would have remembered it." You never know what customers are thinking. And you never know what their fears are. Just handle them one at a time. Make it easy to buy; easy to pay for; and don't spend a lot of time after the sale is done. They want to go just as fast as you want to get to another customer.

OK, they bought it. They're happy.

Next!

What's Your Story?

I have a friend who is a parish priest. He is not what I would call a terrific preacher/speaker. He's not overly articulate, he's not fire and brimstone, and he's not always a real bundle of chuckles from the pulpit. But what he lacks in speaking skills, he makes up with genuine sincerity and personality. Sometimes his words don't come out quite right, like the time he referred to a microwave oven as a "radar range," or when he gave his Labor Day sermon—only to call the holiday "Memorial Day." However, when he talks, everybody listens. He's really got it down. People hang on every word. I've finally figured out why. When he starts his homily, he sets up the topic that he's going to address, and then says, "Let me tell you a story." Everyone listens. Everybody loves to hear a story. Real stories. Not made up stories. Stories they can relate to.

Do you have your own personal stories—stories you can use to make more sales, to sell more instruments? Stories that are more than just a feature-benefit presentation. Stories that will help you sell, stories you can use to follow up a lead, or bring a customer back for the second time. Maybe you could have a couple of great stories why someone should do business with you rather than buying from a major discounter, a catalog, or off the Internet.

One of the best storyteller/salespeople I know is a piano salesperson who has a store in the Northeast. He tells me that often parents come in with a young child (usually a daughter) and ask if he has anything in a used spinet piano. They say they don't want to spend a lot of money if she doesn't stick with it. He asks, "What price range are you looking for?" And then they always go real low. Maybe $500, when the least expensive used piano he has on his floor is $2,000—and new ones are upwards of $3,000. He tells me that when they say $500, he would really like to say "What, are you nuts?" But he doesn't. Instead, he holds his breath. And he tells them a story. I'll give you the *Reader's Digest* version:

He starts by saying, "I know what you mean. I have a daughter myself. But let me tell you about little girls and music. Generally they all have some inherent musical ability. They take lessons. They play for their own enjoyment. They play for their friends. Most of them never make a career out of it. They don't end up playing professionally." Then he says, "You don't care if your daughter never plays Carnegie Hall, do you?" They usually say, "No, we just want her to play for her own enjoyment." And then he says, "But little girls end up becoming big girls. They end up getting married. They move away from home. Sometimes a long way. And when they move, the first thing they want to take with them is their piano. The piano you got for them to take lessons on. Then one day they'll be playing the piano, snow coming down, fire in the fireplace, thinking about all the warm wonderful memories they had growing up playing that same piano when they lived at home. So let me ask you this, do you want a piano for her that will be an heirloom for her children to play on, or a cheap old thing for $500?"

Tears come to their eyes, and that $500 budget starts to reach $5,000. No arm-twisting necessary. No cutting prices to get a deal. The story makes it happen.

When you're talking to a customer in the store or on the phone, and they say that they're going to buy it from your competition down the street or they're going to check the Internet because it could be cheaper, do you have a story about somebody that did just that and has been sorry until this day? Maybe they weren't comparing apples to apples. Maybe it was the product, the service (or lack of), or just an uninformed decision. A story to rationalize why they should buy from you is much better than bad-mouthing the competition or hacking away at price.

But here's the kicker: the stories have to be logical and true. You're not selling snake oil. The stories you use to support your sales presentation have to have credibility and believability. You have to tell them using some integrity as well. Customers don't want to be sold; they want to buy. You help them make a decision. Parables worked for the *Bible*. You can get your own parables to work for you.

Closing Made Easy

Asking for the sale isn't always easy; it's probably the biggest problem salespeople face during the course of a day. When should you ask? How should you try to close? What if the customer says no … ouch! Rejection can sting.

But while you *do* have to ask, it doesn't have to be difficult. If you start asking a customer to buy at the first sign of positive acceptance, your sales can easily increase. You just have to have the guts to say, "Would you like to get it?" or any other variation thereof. Try using a little personality, as well. Getting the customer to like you doesn't hurt; it just gets you in synch with him or her.

During the past few months, I have dealt with a couple of different stock-brokers. With the economy as good as it is, many brokers don't need new business or added business. But I had a rookie broker come to my office with a prospectus and a couple of proposals. His closing line was "OK, the ball's in your court. I don't want to bother you." I didn't want to bother him either, so I took his card, and he left. I never called him back.

The next week, another broker called me. This was someone I had already done business with. I told him I was busy and to call back in a couple of weeks. He said he was coming to my office to drop some stuff off for me. I said that didn't make any sense; I might not be in. He said if I was there, fine—and if not, he would leave the materials. He came over and waited an hour until I arrived. He followed me to my office and said, "This will only take a minute." He showed me a proposal already filled out and said, "Sign here and give me a check." I said I'd think about it. He said, "How much money do you think you'll lose by waiting? I wouldn't be doing my job if I didn't make you aware of this and advise you to invest." I gave him a check. He had the guts to ask, and some decent persistence along with it. He also figured out I didn't want to waste a lot of time thinking about it.

When do you ask a customer to buy? Do you just wait for a customer to say, "I'll take it?" It's amazing how many stores I go into and ask about their merchandise, only to have a salesperson hand me a card as I'm leaving and say, "Let me know when you're ready." Hey, sometimes I don't *know* when I'm ready. Sometimes I have to be pushed. Sometimes I need to be asked several times to buy. Are you clerking or selling? Decide now if you're a salesperson or an order taker.

The funny thing about selling today is that what worked 30 years ago isn't working today. Customers know all the tricks. They know all the closes.

They know when they're getting worked over. They know when you are trying to play with their heads. Forget trying to memorize 75 different closes. It doesn't work. Don't put somebody else's words in your mouth. Use a little personality; make the customer your friend; show them you know your product inside and out; and *ask them to buy it.* You can ask them to buy in a lot of ways:

"OK with you?"
"Want to get it?"
"Should I write it up?"
"Want to take it with you?"
"Would you like it?"

If they say, "No," simply ask, "Why's that?" If they say, "Yes," you're in business.

The most important aspects of closing are knowing when to ask, actually asking, and keeping in synch with your customer at the same time. It's more like being in stride with them, pacing them, and occasionally matching their mannerisms. Think about it like trying to jump aboard a slow-moving freight train. You run alongside it for a bit until you get in stride with the train. Then you reach up with one hand and grab a rung on the ladder while you are still running. Then you reach up with the other hand while you're still running along, and finally jump up and on ... gently. If you don't have the guts to jump up, you get left behind. If you can't match the speed of the train while you are running, you get left behind. If you run too fast and the train is barely moving, you lose your opportunity as well. Selling is exactly the same.

Forget the volumes of books on closing. They won't help if you don't know your products inside and out, if you don't ask the customer to buy, and if you don't use a little decent persistence in case they waiver. Also, you have to treat them with respect and treat them as friends. People are more apt to buy from someone they like. It's that easy.

Closing in the 21st Century

I have been selling most of my adult life. It's amazing how things have changed over the years. Most readers of this column are too young to remember the older sales gurus—J. Douglas Edwards, Cavett Robert, and Zig Ziglar. Later, people like Tom Hopkins, David Sandler, Hank Trisler, and Joe Girard were hot. As soon as they got a foothold, hundreds, if not thousands, more thought that *they* could be gurus, and took up the task of teaching people how to sell. Everybody had different theories, different strategies, and different closing techniques.

Listening to these sales superstars during conventions, sales meetings, and seminars was kind of like going to a revival meeting. But it was not quite like going to church, where the same message is presented week after week, only in a slightly different way. These sales coaches each told us we needed to have a system. Systems like "competitive celling," "neurolinguistic selling," "peak performance selling," and "nonmanipulative selling"—just to name a few.

In these systems they told us you had to do a lot of things, like presenting, qualifying, listening, and managing your time. Then you had to ask the right questions. Questions with names like "Standard Tie-Down," "Tag-On Tie-Down," "Open," "Closed," "Leading," and "Clarifying." After that you had to learn to close. And that wasn't easy either. These disciples of sales gospel stated that you needed an arsenal of closes. Closes like the "Right-Angle Close," the "Impending Event Close," the "Alternative Close," the "Crash-and-Burn Close," the "Similar-Situation Close," the "I'll Think It Over Close," and, of course, the "Ben Franklin Close."

And that was just the beginning.

These worked in the '70s and '80s. I know. I was there. We could slam-dunk more customers into buying something they didn't need (or want) faster than you could say, "Whatcha think, wanna get it?" Man, it was an era to behold. We were slick, crafty, and full of ourselves. Car salespeople dressed like peacocks in heat. They wore shades. Customers shook from fear; they just pulled out their wallets and the salespeople just took what they needed.

Sort of.

But times have changed. Try that today and you'll go broke. If you still have the tapes and workbooks from the sales-hype specialists of bygone years, the best thing you can do is put them in a box and send them to California, where they can be burned in fireplaces and incinerators for additional heat and energy. It just doesn't work anymore, and if you try to use the canned closes, or to put somebody else's words into your mouth, you're going to sound stupid. Customers won't buy—they'll rebel.

Today it takes some personality, product smarts, and honesty—not to mention selling a product that you really believe in. The best thing you can do is find out what works for you and try to capitalize on it. Practice getting customers to smile. Of course, you still have to close—that's not going away. But the trite closes of the past won't work anymore. You have to have the guts to ask people to buy, and you have to do it *nicely*.

Asking (along with a little decent persistence) starts with:
  "Would you like to get it?"
  "OK with you?"
  "If you had this in your home, would you use it?"
  "What can I do to help you make the decision to buy?"
  "Can we write it up?"
  "You're going to love it. How soon would you like it?"
  Or the very simple, "Cash or charge?"

I know, I know, that sounds a little too easy. But selling is no longer hard. J. Douglas Edwards said, "Selling is the lowest-paid easy profession, and the highest-paid hard profession in the whole world." Not true. It can be the highest-paid easy profession if you adapt your own skills, tweak your personality, and develop some sales smarts. And taking those sales smarts to another level starts by knowing your product, believing in your company, getting a customer to like you, finding a need, filling it, and simply having enough nerve to ask them to buy.

Tell you what, test out a few salespeople on your own. Shop for a car. Ask about insurance. Go out to a couple of open houses and see how the real estate people try to get you to buy. If someone says, "Let's see, what old Ben Franklin would do?" then takes out a sheet of paper, draws a line down the middle, and asks you to list all the reasons you would like it versus all the reasons you don't think you would want it, chances are they sold in the '70s. Just tear that piece of paper up into little pieces and leave it on the table. Tell the salesperson to get a life.

Selling today takes a little tact, a little nerve, and a little persistence—then add some integrity and personality. It can be easy. Very easy.

CHAPTER 8:
Store Promotion

It's Not What You Give, It's How You Give It

Not a week goes by when a music store doesn't get a catalog from an advertising specialty company. Salespeople are always knocking on the door, trying to sell trinkets and doodads like pens, key chains, T-shirts or any one of the thousand other products that can be emblazoned with your store name. You can buy those geegaws by the dozen or by the hundred, but are 500 mouse pads or mugs imprinted with your logo really going to bring in a lot more business? It's a tough question.

Advertising specialty products started in the early 1800s, when politicians began printing slogans on buttons and commemoratives to spread their name among voters. That was before radio, TV, and direct mail campaigns. Soon afterward, the American Manufacturing Concern started distributing rulers, yardsticks, paint stirrers, cribbage boards, and paperweights imprinted with store names and advertising messages. By the middle of the 19th century, advertising calendars started to become a common sight in homes and businesses.

When it comes to using advertising specialty products, my best guess is that what will determine how much more business you will do is not *what* you give away but *how* you give it away.

I remember Maury Lindenfeld, a gentleman who had a display at all the home shows, sport shows and mall shows. As you know, many people treat these consumer shows like a game where the winner is the person who came home with the most free stuff. They go around with plastic bags and expect you to drop in a pen, key chain, or whatever. It's like an adult version of trick-or-treating.

Maury would have dozens of ball point pens all nicely positioned in the back of his booth, and as you passed by, he'd have a couple in his hand. If you expressed interest in his product or just a pen, he'd hand you the pen. But when he handed it to you, he'd pull the cap off and keep it in his hand. Then he'd start talking like crazy to find out your name, whether you were a potential customer, and where you lived. You'd stand there with half a pen in your hand waiting for old Maury to release the other part. And he got your attention for a while. He also got more names and numbers than most dealers at the shows.

I remember a less effective music dealer who used to put up a display at local county fairs. He'd give away a key chain with a treble clef on it to anybody who stopped by. He figured that if he gave away a thousand key chains, he'd had a good show. Never mind if he sold anything or did any good prospecting. This advertising strategy didn't make much sense for his business, but the advertising specialty guys sure loved him.

It used to be that prepaid phone cards were one of the biggest giveaways. I know a music dealer who used them to get appointments to show high-priced instruments. He sent a picture of a 10-minute phone card in a letter that explained that he'd give you 10 minutes of talk time, for 10 minutes of your time. Ten minutes was all he wanted to show you a new piano, guitar, band instrument, or drumset. The prepaid cards got him a 65% response rate and resulted in a ton of people actually making appointments.

A freebie has to have perceived value and the customer has to really want it for it to be effective. A throwaway will only reflect badly upon your store and make you look like you didn't care.

The best freebies are ones that give your store lots of free advertising. T-shirts turn your customers into walking billboards for your store. Ball point pens find their way into many people's hands, spreading your store's name as they go. The list of items that can be used to promote your business or yourself is endless. It's up to you to use them effectively.

Some dealers use advertising specialties to bring in more traffic week after week, while others have a tough time just paying the bill for them at the end of the month. It's not what you have imprinted, it's how you use it that matters. You have to have a game plan for how these things are going to bring you more business. Also, if that advertising specialty product you've had imprinted with your store name, slogan, phone number, and address looks like it came from the bottom of a Cracker Jack box, you might want to reconsider what image you are really trying to project. And if that expenditure for those clever, cutesy doodads doesn't bring an increase in sales and more profit to your bottom line in the not-to-distant future, you should probably reconsider before reordering.

The appeal of promotional products lies in the very human need to feel that one is coming out ahead. Everyone likes to get something for free. It's a great concept. Use it to your best advantage.

What Do Your Callers Hear "On Hold"?

How many times a day does your store put callers on hold? Twenty, 50, 100 times, or more? And exactly what do your callers hear during that time? Nothing? Empty space? A local radio station? A CD? A commercial for your store? A commercial *for your competitor's store?*

First of all, if you have nothing—silence—you might be losing calls. In a perfect world, callers should not be put on hold for more than 20 seconds at a time. After a maximum of 20 seconds, someone should ask if the caller can hold longer or get the caller's name and number so someone can call him or her back. Unfortunately, in the real world, we're often put on hold for minutes on end.

When there's only silence, the callers don't know if you've forgotten about them and just hung up. With music playing, at least they know that they're still connected. But this brings up a sticky legal point. If you're using a CD that's being sold publicly, or if you have a radio station playing on hold, you might be violating a law, since you are playing music that you might not be licensed for. ASCAP and various other organizations are getting a little fussy about this, and you might want to check into the legal ramifications before sticking in a CD or turning on the radio. Local nightspots have to pay a fee when they use musicians. It falls under the same guidelines. Be careful. You might end up with a large fine and some bad press.

If you want to play music on hold, consider having some original music written and recorded just for you. Your callers will never hear it anywhere else, and it could become identified with your store. You're in the music business. Maybe you could feature one of your local customers/groups once in a while. Make it a regular thing. Give them a plug.

The worst part of having a local radio station broadcasting on hold is the off chance that your caller could end up listening to a commercial for your competitor. That could really hurt. Particularly if the person is calling for information about a guitar, drum, or any other type of musical instrument, and he or she hears about what your competitor is offering before you come back on the phone. If the commercial involves a price that's lower than what you have to offer, or advertises "sale today only ... hurry down," you might come back on the line to a dial tone.

Another option is to create your own custom-produced messages-on-hold. There are a number of companies around the country that will provide this service for you. One of the companies that does this type of work says: "Not using your on-hold time to promote your business is like having a blank billboard on your property." Their rationale is that if you have 20 callers on hold every day, they represent 450 to 600 people a month you can talk to about your business. But you have to be careful about what you include in your message. You don't want a previous customer calling in to find out that what they purchased is now on sale.

Things like this actually happen. A friend of mine went to a dealer meeting in California on a Friday for two nights. The best room rate he could get was $130. On Friday morning, he called to confirm his room and he heard a commercial, while on hold, advertising the hotel's special "weekend getaway" program rate of $79 a night (based on availability). He called back and requested a reservation at the $79 rate. He was told they had some cancellations and they would be happy to accommodate him. He made the reservation using an initial for his first name and then called back and cancelled the reservation with the higher room rate.

So if you're going to use an on-hold commercial with a price, discount, or current sale information, you'd better watch it. No one wants to find out that instrument he just purchased is now available with a 90 day, no interest payment plan or that there's a factory-authorized sale going on now.

Your own on-hold message can be used to give customers valuable information while they wait. Include directions to your store and the hours you're open. List the brands you carry and your specialties. What services do you offer that your competitors do not? Remind your callers of the benefits of doing business with you.

If you're thinking about putting an on-hold message into your phone system, you might want to call all your competitors and see what they have when put on hold. And then go one better. At the same time you might want to call some of the bigger retailers in your area to see what they do. That will get the wheels churning. Also, call your manufacturers and see what they use. Sometimes the best ideas are inspired from other businesses.

You're dealing with a targeted audience when your callers are on hold. You have their ear. How you fill it is up to you. But it's easy to use your "on-hold" space to bring in more business to your music store. Just use your creativity and you'll see results!

Some Endorsements Are Better Than Others

Former President Bill Clinton and his wife, Hillary, came to Central New York to vacation a few years ago. You may have read about it in the papers or seen it on TV. It's not that Syracuse or Skaneateles is the garden spot of the world, it's because Hillary was getting ready to run for Senator in New York, and she wanted to do some serious Upstate New York schmoozing. She came here for five days, and Bill, Chelsea, and Buddy the dog came with her. They were fundraising like there was no tomorrow. People would line up for hours in the hopes of getting a glimpse of them. Not me. I am not politically motivated. I vote. That's about it.

In fact, I was speaking in New York City for two of those days—totally oblivious to the Clinton-watching. Then one morning, while having coffee in the lobby of the New York Sheraton, I heard "Live from Auburn, New York, with the President and Hillary Clinton" on CNN TV. There really was no escaping it. Instead of playing down the whole thing, I got two tickets for the fundraiser to be held at Mulrooney's Sports Bar on Thursday night. It was right next to my office and I was going to go.

I thought it would be fun to see if President Clinton would accept a copy of our video on "How to Find Gigs That Pay Big Bucks." This is a video we produced for aspiring musicians on how to get out of the garage and into the world of good paying jobs. It is sponsored by the American Federation of Musicians, along with some of the top musical instrument manufacturers. It's selling well through catalogs and magazines, and on the Internet. It is also available in music stores. It's for musicians who want to get better work. Bill Clinton is a saxophone player. At the time, he was a year away from leaving office. Get the picture? A picture of Bill and our video would be nice.

Now getting to Bill and Hillary was not an easy chore. Not with 100,000 other people vying for the same two seconds of face time. So here's a little breakdown of President Clinton, the video, and our brush with history on one Thursday evening at Mulrooney's Sports Bar in Syracuse:

6:45 P.M. We wait in line outside Mulrooney's to show ID, get frisked, go through a metal detector, and go into the bar. Outside 4,000 people can't come within two blocks. There are sharpshooters on the roofs of buildings.

Secret Service people are everywhere. We feel like real big deals—flashing our ID and going through the door.

7:00 P.M. We are inside. Food and drinks are free. Joe Rainone, the owner of Mulrooney's, is congenial, friendly, smiling, and very nervous.

7:30 P.M. More waiting. More drinking. Joe has this place running like the motor of a well-tuned car. Everybody has food. They bring it to you if you can't get to the bar or to the roast beef tables.

8:00 P.M. We wait. The crowd now is so deep that it's almost hard to breathe. My hands are sweating and the shrink-wrap on the videos in my hand is starting to melt. I don't want anything more to drink. My stomach is in knots. I wonder if I can come within 40 feet of the President.

8:30 P.M. Still waiting. People are starting to get antsy. I make friends with one of the Secret Service people. He tells me where the President and First Lady are going to be. They are not going to actually "work the bar and shake hands with everybody." They are going to one spot, say a few words, and leave. I have one of my better friends with me—Pat Judycki. Pat is also one of my *bigger* friends. His job is to block for me, shoot pictures with a camera in each hand, and help get me to the Chief Executive. My plan is to give the President one of our videos, hope we get a picture of him taking it, and get some press on it.

8:45 P.M. Bill and Hillary arrive. Three hundred people struggle to get a glimpse, a touch, a handshake. There are gifts for the President in shopping bags. It looks like a shower. The President heads our way. Hillary is working the crowd like a pro.

8:47 P.M. Pandemonium. The people in the back of the restaurant have no chance of reaching the President. We are in front, right where they are coming by. Mr. President waves to one of the waitresses standing up on a booth. She tries to shake is hand. He motions her to jump down. She jumps, he catches her. Flashes pop all over the place. I think to myself, "I've seen this movie." His charisma is like nobody I've ever seen. He could charm the pants off of anybody. (Insert joke here).

8:48 P.M. The President is in front of me. Pat is blocking and snapping. I shake Bill's hand, and thrust the video toward him. He sees the title. He says, "Who's the video for?" I respond, "For aspiring musicians who want to get in the big time." He says, "That's cool; I want it." I said, "It's yours," and he's pushed away to another dozen, frenzied, handshaking well wishers. I am beside myself.

8:50 p.m. President Clinton is shaking hands with people just to get away from them. The Secret Service really has their work cut out for them. I then realize, *the video is still in Clinton's hand. He's showing it to people.*

8:55 p.m. Hillary goes up to a makeshift stand where there's a microphone. President Clinton follows her. She starts to speak. Bill's heard it before, *so he starts to read the back panel of the video,* while Hillary is talking. This is amazing. Cameras are clicking and flashes are going off like it's the Fourth of July.

9:05 p.m. Hillary's done; the President addresses the crowd. He says, "I've just received a video called *How to Find Gigs That Pay Big Bucks.* It might come in handy when I leave office." I am thrilled beyond belief.

9:15 p.m. President and Mrs. Clinton make their way out of the restaurant. She passes me. She sees the other video. She says "Got one for me?" She comes over, I give her the video, put my arm around her, she smiles, and I get the picture. Another brush with history. Two hundred other people can't come within 20 feet. I'm ringside. Now I've got goosebumps. I am so happy I can't stand it.

9:20 p.m. Bill leaves the restaurant, Hillary stays to shake more hands. I hear him mumble something about the video again, so I thrust my card at him to let him know where it came from. Somebody throws another card at him to autograph. Seconds later, I get my card back with *Bill Clinton* signed over the front. I yell, "*Hey Mr. President, what the heck is this? You need the card to see where the video came from!*" He yelled back, "Then you better have another card with you!" I did. I gave it to him. And in five seconds, he was gone.

9:25 p.m. I feel like I've just run 10 plays against the Minnesota Vikings. I am beat. The President of the United States talked about our video for the national press, Hillary and I had our picture taken together, and Bill's autograph is on my business card. It is a night to remember.

FRIDAY MORNING. Our "Gigs Video and President Clinton" makes the local papers, the business journals, *The New York Times,* and *Bloomberg News Radio.* It's fed to the national TV news networks and calls from radio talk shows are coming in.

I can't think of anything bigger than meeting the President. Maybe meeting the Pope. But I admit, I downplayed it in the beginning, and now will remember it for the rest of my life. I was thrilled to have the chance of a lifetime. And getting the President as an endorser for our video was pretty cool as well!

Outside Piano Sales Events: Do They Still Work?

I've heard that college sales, armory sales, and piano sales in hotels and convention centers, at one time, accounted for more than 35% of all piano business. Sometimes it seems you couldn't pick up a paper in a major metro area without seeing an ad for these types of events. We hear stories of piano dealers who gross hundreds of thousands of dollars at just one of these three-day events. Some of them generate more business than many dealers do in a year. I wanted to know if this is factual, and also wanted to know if they still bring in as much revenue as the numbers claim.

These outside sales are not anything new. I remember truck operations 40 years ago where a dealer would run a classified ad reading, "Wanted: Responsible party to take over payments on spinet piano." Then a couple of guys would come into town, drive their truck up to every respondent's house, and hammer them into buying a Story & Clark (or whatever they had at the time) piano, by telling them whatever they needed to hear. These guys were slick. My favorite part of the pitch was the way they convinced customers to purchase a new bench. "We repossessed the piano from these folks, but felt bad and wanted to leave them something for the money they put in, so we left them the bench," they would say. "We can give you a brand new bench for just a few hundred bucks or so."

Then 30 years ago, the sales were moved into empty storefronts and hotel rooms. There was a little more integrity, and with some decent hard work and creative advertising, a dealer could do pretty well. But they still weren't achieving the numbers you see today.

Bob Furst was the first person I can remember who tried out the college sale idea. He was from the Los Angeles area, and to his credit, probably was more inventive than any 12 piano salespeople you could name. He was ahead of his time. I don't even know if he's still around, but he had more ways to sell a piano than anyone I had ever seen. He would write books on selling pianos and could probably sell his print material by the pound. He knew a ton of information on the subject. His idea was simple. He would give a college or university some pianos to use for a semester or two at no charge. And at the end of the loaner term, he would bring in a truckload of pianos to sell at the college, advertising "pianos used at (whatever) college." Now maybe there were other people who had the same idea, but Bob Furst sure exploited it. He would get the alumni list and a demographic list of potential buyers. Bob made sure to send out mailers to them and combined this with advertisements in the local paper. The results were amazing. He would sell pianos like crazy.

Tony Siciliano picked up where Bob Furst left off. His company is National Piano Institute (NPI) Marketing services, also in Los Angeles, which does these outside event piano sales for dealers around the country. He's been doing it for years. I have heard the results from some of his sales have been very profitable and moved a lot of pianos.

So I decided to give Tony a call, along with about 40 other dealers nationwide, to find out how successful outside sales events have recently been. I called dealers from Hawaii to New York, and I talked to dealers from just about every major metro market and their surrounding towns. Piano dealers are an interesting group of people and the good ones are aggressive and will latch onto anything they can use. When I got them talking, I asked them if they did outside pianos sales at places like colleges and armories, how they have done in the past, and how they are doing today. Here are my findings:

Tony at NPI said that his sales are still doing well. The dealers that may run into a snag sometimes forget the basic elements of what makes these sale events work.

Kathi Kretzer in West Palm Beach, Florida, said they may not be working quite as well, but the economy has changed and the business is still out there.

Dale Matthies in Honolulu, Hawaii, decided to take a different route and places more emphasis on outside clinics and setting up on weekends at warehouse clubs like Sam's Club and Costco. They hold down the cost, and he goes back several times a year. He says it's a major part of his business.

Jim Trimper in Buffalo, New York, hates putting out $5,000 or more just in moving costs, so he concentrates on doing more events in the store. The gross is not nearly as high, but it is much easier.

Dealers like Mike Vaccaro in Kansas City, Kansas, and Mike Greene in San Diego, California, still do them regularly with excellent results.

Bill Boyce of Raleigh, North Carolina, and Tampa, Florida, goes to convention centers, fairgrounds, or any other place that can hold a lot of his pianos and draw a crowd. Bill has ideas for piano sales that most dealers have never even heard of, and most of them work. It's a numbers game.

Lamar Roach also does outside events for piano dealers. His company specializes in outside event sales for Steinway dealers. He maintains that, if you stick to the principles that make them work, you'll do well. Danny Saliba at Steinway in Dallas, Texas, confirms that.

Maurice Unis who also does some of the Steinway events says the same. In fact just about all the Steinway dealers I talked with still produce tremendous numbers.

Dealers who don't believe in the promotion, take sides against those that do. Our clipping service came through with an ad from Lentine's Music in Akron, Ohio, whose ad had a box with a quote from the *Larry Fine Piano Book*. It read: "Piano Shoppers don't be misled! Sometimes a team of professional high-pressure salespeople is hired to stage 'armory sales,' 'university sales,' or sales named after a local concert or festival. Dealers who don't participate in these mega-sales can often offer you a better deal, and virtually offer a more pleasant shopping experience." I don't know if Larry Fine liked having his name used, but it's obvious that these outside event piano sales stir things up. There still seems to be a lot of piano business out there.

I found that there are some common denominators that make these events successful. One is the location. It's got to be an easy-to-get-to spot with free, convenient parking. Second, the sale has to be believable. You can't use the same handle time after time and expect the same results. Third, a good mailing list is a must. Tony Siciliano says that the right demographics are important, and he spends as much time researching and coming up with the right list (a service which he provides to dealers), as he does planning the entire event. The mailer itself has to be creative and clever, and the letter or card needs to generate interest.

About 60% or more of the sales at these events seem to come from appointments. The direct mail piece urges appointments, and the staff at the piano stores need to get on the phone a week before the event to ask for referrals, try to get past prospects to come to the event, and generally talk up the sale to everyone they know. All the dealers I talked to say the best results come when they use a "greeter." Prospects and customers coming to the sale have to fill out an appointment/prospect card first, and have a salesperson accompany them into the sale area. The other key to making these sales work is a competent, hard-working sales staff. They have to know how to close. This is no place for clerks or mild-mannered salespeople wannabees. If you can't close, then you aren't going to make a sale.

The dealers who run these sales successfully spend a lot of money on the event. It costs a lot for moving, advertising, buying a list, mailing, bringing in "hired guns" (if there is not enough sales staff), renting a location, and on and on. The dealers who have a couple of successful sales and try to cut back expenses by moving the event into the store, never seem to achieve the success as they did when they went to a remote location and created excitement and urgency.

At these outside event piano sales, there seem to be some similar prospects/ customers/people who show up at every sale. There will always be someone who has no intention of buying, but will play every piano nonstop (particularly the most expensive grands) to show off how well they play, while annoying everybody, and then they'll leave. Someone will always come in, hit the very last key on a piano and say, "Why does this sound so bad?" At least once a customer will come in and say they have to "ask their friend/tuner/acquaintance/teacher before they can even think about buying a piano" and never come back. There will be someone who has just bought a piano and only comes in to make sure they got a good deal. They will then tell everyone within earshot that their piano is better than what is displayed on the floor. Look out for these people. On the other hand, there are many more people who come in with cash or good credit, who are legitimate prospects, and will spend money when given a good reason to. They will come up with the cash or credit if perceived value exceeds price. That's what makes these sales work.

Outside Piano Sales Events: The Customer

It's been a long time since I actually sold a piano. I wondered if the customers who shop for a piano at college sales, armory sales, and warehouse club sales are the same type of customers who were looking for one 20 years ago. This was the question I posed to piano dealers and salespeople around the country regarding these outside sales events. What I found was the answer is both yes and no.

I talked with Larry Fresch, district manager of Geneva International; John Phanco of Florida Keyes in Daytona Beach, Florida; Art Olson of Artistic Pianos in Encinidas, California; and Bob Zadel, a former industry executive who is now with Desert Piano in Palm Springs, California. They all agreed that today's perimeter piano sale customer who walks into a store event is a lot more educated than the customers of years past. They are more knowledgeable because of tools such as the Internet, which allows them to compare features and prices at their fingertips. They know there are other options besides acoustic pianos. They know that digitals exist, they know the prices of grand pianos, and often they are aware of various makes and models long before they walk through the door.

Larry Fresch pointed out that many piano salespeople take the path of least resistance when selling a piano. They would rather sell a piano at a lesser price, with a smaller margin in a quicker manner, instead of going back to the basics. He says a better salesperson would take a piano apart, explain the features and benefits and close a piano sale and make a decent profit. That's where mid-range pianos take a real hit, he says. The novice salesperson offers only two choices: really cheap or really good.

John Phanco mentioned that digitals have really overshadowed acoustic pianos in his area. Years ago digital pianos were nonexistent, and electronic pianos sounded nothing like acoustic pianos. Now people are aware of the price ranges and features and sometimes don't even want to look at a vertical or grand piano. When customers arrive in the store, or at the outside event sale, with preconceived thinking about piano models Art Olson says he re-educates the customer. He says that by taking extra time with the customer he sees a better gross result. The salespeople agree that, in order to make decent money in the piano industry, you have to win customers over with your personality and your sales presentations must be well thought out.

Bob Zadel mentioned that his selling area is smaller in scope, but has a lot of upscale shoppers who will spend money for higher priced pianos.

When I asked him if that means they don't dicker, he told me the story of an older couple who came into the store and fell in love with a $32,000 grand piano. The lady went over to the piano and asked, "What's the best you can do on this piano?" Bob replied, "The best I can do is $32,000." To which the woman yelled over to her husband: "We have a smart ass here, Honey." I guess people want to negotiate over a piano purchase, no matter what the price is or how bad they want it. He also told me about a gentleman who came in and said he already had three prices on a certain piano and wanted to know their best price. The salesperson asked what the prices were that he had already found. The gentleman said he wouldn't tell him, so the salesperson said, "I didn't know we were playing poker."

I guess haggling over price is the name of the game. All in all, I found that the outside event piano sales and specific promotion sales still sell a lot of inventory. And almost everybody agrees that you have to fight harder to get a sale and lean on the customer a little more.

Turning Customers into Torchbearers

Wouldn't it be great if every customer who ever bought an instrument from your music store told 10 more people to do the same? What if every person who left your store raved so much about your instruments, lessons, and service that they turned into evangelists for your store? Think it's impossible? While you're thinking about whether it's impossible or not, consider the people who wear the Nike "swoosh" symbol on their hats and shirts, and the Harley-Davidson fanatics who tattoo the name of their favorite bike on their arms, chest, and other extremities.

These people aren't just customers who have an interest in a product or store. These people have a belief, and one person with a belief is equal to a force of 99 who have an interest. Have you ever run into a devoted Macintosh user and asked why they prefer a Mac over a PC? They can be one-person PR programs. These people have a passion for the product.

To turn your customers into torchbearers for your instruments and your store, you first must have something for them to rave about. Creating a "great, best-there-is" place to buy or "out-of-the-ordinary" service to back up what you sell is the first step to turning customers into evangelists for you and your store. And you'll never get a customer to tell how much they love your inventory or your store unless you have a passion for it yourself. If you have a love for what you're doing and an understanding of your customers' needs, that's the start of a cause where your customers can help wave your flag for you.

Few people want to be associated with a mediocre store or a less-than-average product. They don't want their friends to know they were manipulated into buying something, and they don't want their peers to find out that they made a buying decision, then received shoddy service or settled for poor quality.

Take this little quiz:

Do you feel you carry the finest, "absolutely, without a doubt" best instruments on the market today?

Do you feel that no one can touch your place of business for value, service, and inventory selection?

Does everyone in your store help create an environment where customers feel they have immediately come to the right place and that they are making the right decision?

Do you have a "Customer Advisory Council" of your own, where you listen to customers' needs, let them help evaluate new instruments, and make them feel like they're part of your team?

Do you pursue your existing customers to bring them to a higher level of commitment?

Do you handle every customer complaint, question, or dissatisfaction like it is the only one of the day and that the sales to another 100 people will depend on it?

If a customer tells you that the instrument he purchased a week ago can be purchased cheaper down the street, do you rationalize your store and service value versus price, and make him a believer, or does he sulk out of the store vowing never to come back?

If you answered "no" to any of the questions, it's going to be difficult to create torchbearers and evangelists for your music store. If the answers are all "yes," you're on your way. If the answer is a huge, emphatic "YES!" you're probably there and your customers are already spreading the word.

Have you ever seen the commercials for Troy-Bilt rototillers and grass cutters on TV? Troy-Bilt recruits owners of their machines to help sell their products. The owners don't actually "sell" the products, but they endorse them if a potential customer calls. And Troy-Bilt suggests that prospects call these people to see if they're happy. To answer questions. To give advice. These volunteer salespeople are part of the company's "Good Neighbor" program. Troy-Bilt recruits them at the time of purchase by offering them a discount or free attachment. Troy-Bilt owners are evangelists about their machines and like to spread the good news. These torchbearers support the company by providing credible information to potential customers.

Applebee's restaurants train their servers to continually ask customers if everything is OK; if there is anything else they can do; if there is anything else they need. Not just once, but several times during the course of a meal. If there is a problem, the manager comes out, apologizes, and gets involved. If everything is not quite right, they make it right, and there is no check—the meal is free. The manager asks the customer to come back again and give them another chance. They turn an unhappy dinner guest into a torchbearer by having them tell all their friends ... not that the meal was bad, but how the employees went out of their way to rectify it, to make them happy.

A local carwash has a neat way of creating torchbearers. They know the names of all their best customers and keep them on a computer database according to license number. As the car is pulling up, they run the license plate number on their computer which tells them the name of the customer, and how many times the car has been in during the past few months. They make sure that the customers are called by name when they come in. Then they will comp a car wash every once in a while. You never know. Once in a while they will say, "It's OK ... it's on us ... come back again." When the customer thanks them for the freebie, they say, "No problem, just send another customer our way. We want more people like you." It's a personal touch that no one else offers. They almost have a cult following.

Don't forget your employees. One person with a bad attitude can bring your whole company down. Think twice about anybody who is not proud to work for your store. Employees are torchbearers too. They're helping to promote your cause. Find the right people and make sure they're the right fit for your team.

With everybody carrying the torch, you won't have to spend thousands of dollars on weekly advertising just to get people through your door. Your employees, customers, and all the people they know can help do it for you.

Even if You're Small You Can Still Act Big

I have found that sometimes the smaller the store, the more difficult it is to get information, or reach the owner, unless he or she actually answers the phone. Some of the calls I made were interesting. Some were excellent. Some were depressing. I called a music store in Memphis, and here is the actual conversation:

Store: XXX and XXX (I don't want to use the real name because I really don't want to embarrass anyone.)

Me: Hi, this is Bob Popyk. Is XXX (the owner) there?

Store: Who did you say you were again?

Me: Bob Popyk … It's spelled P-O-P-Y-K

Store: Is he expecting your call?

Me: I really don't know, but if I say, "no," does that mean I can't talk to him?

Store: Hang on.

Store: (After three minutes on hold) Where did you say you were from again?

Me: I didn't.

Store: Well, could I tell him? Were you looking to buy something?

Me: I didn't know he was screening his calls. Tell him I do a column for *Music Trades* magazine.

Store: Oh, OK, let me see if I can get him.

Store: (After another two minutes on hold) He's not here.

Me: Can I leave a message to have him call me.

Store: You're better off calling back. He's pretty busy, and his desk is a mess. He might not see it.

You would be absolutely amazed how unprofessional some of these smaller stores I called were. I got the immediate impression that this owner is being chased by creditors, is late on his rent payment, and is being beaten up by suppliers. If you're in a town where you have to compete with the bigger guys, you might want to rethink how your staff answers the phone. Image is important.

Here's another conversation I had when calling a different store:

Store: Thanks for calling XXX music!

Me: Hi, this is Bob Popyk. Can I speak with XXX?

Store: Sure. Let me get him. And just in case he asks, can I get your name again? I want to make sure I have it right to show I'm doing my job.

Me: It's Bob Popyk. Spelled P-O-P-Y-K.

Store: OK, just one second.

Store: (After 5 seconds). I see he's got a customer. I can take your number and make sure he will call you back, or is there something I might be able to help you with? I've been here for a while and know a lot about the inventory, lessons, and pricing. Just trying to save you time.

Me: OK, let me give you my number and little about what I'd like to talk with him about. You can pass it on to him.

I got the impression from this call that everyone in the store was knowledgeable and that it was a fun place to do business. Just the conversation alone sounded like it was a no-hassle environment.

If you're a small store you can learn a lot from stores that might be bigger than you. And this lesson doesn't have to be found just in the music business. A while back, I was reading about McDonald's in *USA Today*. They were experimenting with renting videos. Blockbuster is worried. So what? The point is that even the giants don't stand still, and while McDonald's is in the food business, they're also in the convenience business. Frankly, it may well be a loss leader, but if it drives additional traffic into the store, that's good. People were able to rent a video in one location and return it to another. That's actually brilliant! They tested this idea in several major markets.

There are a lot of interesting trends in retail that may well set the pace for others to follow. Remember, you're in the life-enhancement business, not just the music business. You just have to keep up with what's going on in the world, and figure out how you can implement it if you're a smaller business.

Advertising on the Cheap

Not all music stores have the advertising budgets of Guitar Center, Brook Mays, or Schmidts. Because of the high costs, many smaller stores find it tough to include any kind of major media in their advertising budget on a regular basis. Advertising has changed. No longer are there three or four local stations on your TV set. Now you have hundreds of channels to choose from; and if you want to make an impact by advertising on TV, you either need a large checkbook or a good crystal ball.

Your car radio can have 25 stations or more, with every type of format possible. Reaching that drive-time audience is a real trick because not only are the stations with the highest market share expensive, XM and Sirius are scooping up market share by adding listeners daily with no commercial interruption.

And the local newspapers are no bargain either. Advertising rates are way up, while readership is down. So where does a small store spend its advertising dollars today? Good question. I'm not sure what all the answers are, but after talking to a number of high-profile advertising people, they agreed that having a great mailing list (both e-mail and snail mail) is a good start. The trick here is to come up with something clever to get your readers to want to learn more, and to put your name on the top of their minds when they are thinking about buying a musical instrument.

This is not new. I would guess that most of the readers of this column don't remember Burma Shave, a shaving cream from many decades ago. They were the epitome of inexpensive advertising, and Burma Shave was synonymous with shaving cream for years and years. They didn't have much money to advertise. They didn't have a mailing list. Computers weren't even thought of back then. Here's what they did way back in 1925:

A young fellow by the name of Allan Odell came up with a great sales idea that he showed to his father, Clifford. He suggested using small, wooden roadside signs to pitch their product, Burma-Shave, a relatively unknown brushless shaving cream. His dad wasn't wild about the idea but eventually gave Allan $200 to give it a try.

It didn't take long for sales to soar. Soon Allan and his brother Leonard were putting up signs all over the place. At first the signs were pure sales pitch, but as the years passed they found their sense of humor extending to safety tips and pure fun. And some good old-fashioned down home wisdom, much of it obtained from contests.

At the height of their popularity there were 7,000 Burma-Shave signs stretching across America. The familiar white on red signs, grouped by fours, fives and sixes, were as much a part of a family trip as irritating a family member from the back seat of the car. You'd read first one, then another, anticipating the punch line on number five and the familiar Burma-Shave on the sixth.

The signs cheered us during the Depression and the dark days of World War II. But things began to change in the late '50s. Cars got faster and super-highways were built to accommodate them. The fun little signs were being replaced by huge, unsightly billboards. With the diminishing countryside and the expansion of America, Burma Shave could no longer keep up. By 1963 they were all gone. As befits such an important part of American culture, one set is preserved by the Smithsonian Institution. It reads:

Shaving brushes
You'll soon see 'em
On a shelf
In some
Museum
Burma-Shave

And in the interest of providing some historical advertising education, here are a few more from the side of the road:

If these
Signs blur
And bounce around
You'd better park
And walk to town
Burma-Shave

You can beat
A mile a minute
But there ain't
No future
In it
Burma-Shave

Sleep in a chair
Nothing to lose
But a nap
At the wheel
Is a permanent snooze
Burma-Shave

It spreads so smooth
It shaves so slick
It feels
Like velvet
And it's quick
Burma-Shave

His line was smooth
But not his chin
He took her out
She took him in
To buy some
Burma-Shave

Drinking drivers
Enhance their
Chance
To highball home
In an ambulance
Burma-Shave

OK, got the idea? It's a bunch of signs by the side of the road. A few lines to get your attention, and then the Burma-Shave name. Consistent advertising with brand identification. The Burma-Shave people rented the space for practically nothing from farmers on busy highways. Passersby looked forward to reading them.

Now let's fast forward to today. You are not going to put signs by the side of the road. Local ordinances would probably fine you plenty, or landowners would want a small fortune. But you do need a hook to get people to read your e-mail or direct mail. Something so your reader doesn't instantly delete it, report it for spam, or throw it in the wastebasket.

I didn't think ANY business could coerce me into opening their e-mail, or opening their envelope, especially when I knew it was advertising. But as technology evolves, I guess I have bought into plenty of solicitations as a customer, especially when I think there is something in it for me. For example, Pier I has special incentives and coupons only available online. CompUSA has last-minute specials only available online. ET Wright shoes doesn't normally discount, but you might find a coupon available in their monthly e-mail. And as far a regular mail goes, Northwest Airlines will send out a highly discounted coupon to selected lists every few months or so, so you want to open any envelope from them that might contain some serious savings.

Here's how to determine what works, and what doesn't: What e-mail advertising have you opened and read, and what have you deleted? What envelopes have you tossed, and which ones have you read? If something either piqued your curiosity, got you to respond, or made you pull out your credit card, make a note of it. After a few weeks, check your list of things that grabbed your attention, and go and do likewise.

Radio, TV, and newspaper advertising are expensive shotgun approaches to mass audiences. E-mail and direct-mail is a rifle shot to a select a list of people who may have already done business with you, are apt to do business with you, or know people who will do business with you. You just need to find a clever way to grab their attention. Like Burma-Shave did, only with direct-mail and e-mail, instead of signs on the side of the road.

Don't Let a Crisis Drive
Your Advertising Decisions

I had a phone call from a music dealer in the Midwest recently. He has a small music store in a town of about 100,000 people and a shopping population about twice that number.

Business had slowed down, to the point where he was really getting concerned, so he decided to do some advertising. He wanted to "reach out and touch someone" as he put it, so he "reached out" and no one was there. He wanted to do something quick, so he hastily put together an ad for his local paper and ran some drive-time radio spots. (He heard that was the best thing to do to get results).

The results turned out to be negligible. I think the word "quick" had a lot to do with the dismal return on investment. Business gets soft, customers stop coming in, and we immediately "have to do some advertising." But where, and how much?

I did my own research on how to reach people who would be considered good prospects to buy musical instruments and accessories from a small store. It looks as though the smaller dealers are going to need a big checkbook and a bigger crystal ball, because there seems to be no consistency any more. It's not easy. To begin with, the newspapers aren't always a great medium these days. Readership is down in many parts of the country (but ad rates are up), and the trend is spiraling downward. (I did notice, though, that throwaway Pennysavers have more music store ads lately.)

Drive-time radio is a tough bet, because there are about 20 stations with different formats in most major markets competing for listening share, and, while nobody was paying attention, XM and Sirius radio took a foothold. You don't have to listen to commercials on Howard Stern (Sirius) or Frank's Place (XM), and the numbers of listeners are increasing daily on Satellite radio. Forget TV. With cable channels now in the hundreds, market share for any individual station has gone into tilt. And with DVR and TIVO, viewers can skip commercials at will.

I looked through my local *Yellow Pages* for listings under "Music Stores." The placements are smaller and smaller. Unfortunately, there is a painful decline in the use of the *Yellow Pages*, because countless free Internet sites offer the same information and update more frequently.

E-mail marketing is still going on, but spam-induced antagonism about having mailboxes stuffed with unsolicited messages brought that medium down quickly. Today, we also have blogging and Google to contend with.

Just think about these various streams that have entered our society and you realize connecting with our desired audience is a challenge that is increasingly difficult, demanding, and elusive. There are many more ways to advertise now than ever before. And unless you are one of the major big-box music chains, using more than one or two media is starting to become unaffordable as well.

Here is a consensus of opinions from four large advertising agencies, who serve smaller retail operations, on approaching your use of advertising dollars. I've boiled them down to five main points:

1) Never let a crisis affect your advertising decisions. When you "have to do something immediately" to bring business in, it sometimes results in irrational actions.
2) Come up with an entire advertising and marketing plan, not just a one-shot approach to temporary salvation.
3) Don't get your arm twisted into making a buying decision. The "we're running out of advertising inventory" doesn't make it today. There are just too many ways to go and things to consider in buying advertising.
4) Focus on just one type of buyer at a time. If you want to move pro-audio equipment, don't tie it in with drum sets and music stands. It's rifle shots, not buckshot that will get a better return.
5) Don't quit. Don't give up. Persistence pays off. Advertising is a "what medium," not a "why medium." Keep trying to see what works. Don't try to figure out why. Then, once an approach works, keep doing it. People who didn't catch it the first time might be touched by it the next time around. Persistence is about planning. Failure is usually the result of quickly made decisions.

Do You Advertise "Great Customer Service," or Is It a Given?

The music business has changed drastically over the past few years. Not long ago, we didn't have to worry about the Internet, major chains, low priced imports, and big-box discount stores.

Years ago the biggest worry was another small dealer opening up down the street, or maybe competing with the Sears catalog. Now Guitar Center comes to town, more and more websites are popping up selling instruments near cost, Target has started stocking more instruments, and the competition seems never ending. It's getting tougher and tougher for smaller dealers to compete. Heck, make that any size dealer.

I really thought about what smaller businesses go through to compete when I took two of my cars in for service the other day. I have a few classic cars (if you can call 1991 Buick Reatta convertibles classic) and a two-year-old Lexus RX330. I took one of the Buicks in to a huge local GM dealer because of a wiring problem. At the same time I took the Lexus in to a small Lexus dealer close by, to repair a front-end problem.

The Lexus service department gave me a loaner, told me that they could give me a "courtesy warranty" on the front end (even though I didn't buy the car there), and suggested a synthetic oil change. The total charge was $55.95. At the mega-dealer, they told me the cost would be $397.50 for the wiring module, didn't have time for anything else, couldn't give me a loaner, and told me the car would be done by the end of the day … maybe.

At the end of the day, the mega-dealer service guys couldn't find the problem, charged me $95 to replace a taillight bulb, which I could have done myself, and said to leave it there for another two days. I picked the car up, told them I would work on the wiring myself, and told them about the Lexus experience. Their comment was, "Oh sure, they're Lexus."

OK, this story is not about selling pianos, trumpets, guitars, or drum sets, but it is about a small dealership in a big field that probably doesn't crank out a lot of sales each day. The small Lexus dealer competes using personal attention and excellent customer service, without any kind of heavy discounting. Its people really get to know their customers. It doesn't advertise great service—customers expect it.

On the other hand, the GM mega-dealership delivers a lot of iron over the curb each day, probably selling cars by the hour, if not the minute. It doesn't have time for individualized "let's see how I can help you" service. At the mega-dealer, you are a number not a name. You are a short-term profit source rather than a long-term customer.

If you are a small music dealer, you have a lot going in your favor. You can get to know most (if not all) of your customers personally. You can make loaners available if someone's instrument breaks down before a gig, offer music instruction from qualified teachers, and take the time to find out who your customers' friends and relatives are, and try to get them into your store. Great customer service is expected from small shops.

Think about the mega-stores you visit where you never see the same salespeople working there two visits in a row. How readily will they help you with a problem?

I think the secret to success for small and mid-size (and even larger) music dealers is to remember what the function of your business actually is. If you think it is to make a profit, you are wrong. Making a profit is the goal. The function of your business should be to create and maintain customers.

Once you start to confuse the function with the goal, you have a problem. Exceptional customer service is expected. You just have to live up to it, and you have to concentrate on creating customers. Not just you as the owner, everyone in the store has to help. The big box and discount music stores can afford to spend tens of thousands on advertising to get customers through the door. Smaller stores can't. You have to find customers one at a time, and the best way is to get all your staff involved.

Make sure everyone you employ has their own business cards to give out to everyone they come in contact with. Stay in touch with your customers with regular personalized mailings, both e-mail and snail mail. Send thank-you notes. Call customers on the phone once in a while. Capitalize on quality lesson programs. Bring in the recreational musicians your competition overlooks.

What Is Your "Event of the Day"?

One of the easiest ways to compete with the Internet and to keep your advertising costs in line is to bring people into your store regularly by having "participatory activities." These are daily events to bring in store traffic. The more events during the week, the better. More and more music stores are getting on board with this. There are a lot of ways to fill your calendar with different activities. Class lessons are high on the list. Concerts and clinics should be done regularly. But there are dozens (if not hundreds) of other things you can do to bring people in on a regular basis without spending huge bucks on advertising or store promotion.

Having an "advisory board" might be one idea. Several music stores already do this. They ask their best customers to be part of the (your store name) Music Advisory Committee. For this, selected customers get to be on a special e-mail list, and once a month, these customers are invited to see instruments that are new and asked to give an opinion. Advisory committee members get refreshments, schmooze with their friends, and get a special discount if they want to buy the instrument. These customers also get to suggest people who may be interested in purchasing that new piano, keyboard, guitar, drumset, amp, PA system, brass instrument, or whatever, even if it is not on their priority list. Advisory Committee members also get a plaque for their wall at home (to impress their friends) and maybe a coffee mug or store t-shirt. There is no limit to how many people you can have on your "advisory committee."

George Hines of George's Music sends out postcards to Very Important Players (VIPs). Customers who spend more than $300 become VIP's and are entitled to accessories' discounts. VIP nights could bring in a ton of business. Most store events are free, but some music stores occasionally charge for an activity night. It could be an instructional clinic for jazz guitar players, where people spend $5 each, or a fundraiser for a local charity featuring a well-known local musician. Whether you charge a few bucks or do it for free, the key is getting people in the door. It could be something as simple as a local psychologist talking about the healing powers of music, or how learning to play an instrument could make your kid smarter.

Preferred Customer Appreciation Nights are something else that could be done once a month. The thing here is not to have too many people on one night. Space it out. If you get too many people, it is going to be tough to sell if you can't spend quality time with the better prospects. It's easier to spend quality time with fewer people for bigger sales. The nice part here is that it can be done after the store is closed with soda, wine and cheese, coffee, and snacks. It can be done later in the evening. Customer Appreciation Nights should be social events rather than trying to ram-rod business. Sales will happen. You just need bodies to talk to and people who have an interest in what you sell.

Concert nights should be planned carefully. Again, too many people can hamper sales. Target your audience carefully. It would be good to have an event calendar so people can see what you are having on what days. They can pick and choose, and it's easier to send out a whole month at a glance, or pick up a copy at your store, than it is to keep resending postcards or other direct mail pieces. That's where e-mail really comes into play. You can keep hammering away so people will expect to hear about the next event at your store with reminders sent a few days before.

To keep these events full, make sure your staff gets the e-mail and physical address of every person they talk to. This should even be from the people who call in for info. (Just tell them they will follow-up the information they were looking for by e-mail.) Getting phone numbers is great, because you can call them once in awhile about something special and ask them to bring their friends.

You can't have a store party on the Internet. You can't have an in-store clinic online. Participatory activities are going to play a big part in independent music stores from here on out. It could be "Name That Tune for Cash Prizes," or a contest to see who plays the best after 10 lessons. It could be a free guitar restringing night, or an instrument "petting zoo" for school children to decide what instrument would be best for them. You're only limited by your imagination. People will come if you make it interesting. And if they are really interested, they may buy something.

How's Your Customer Credibility Factor?

Have you taken a look at the ads in the newspaper recently? Here's a list of what they're saying: "Sale," "Inventory Clearance," "Save Up to XX Percent," "Closeout," and "Hurry ... Offer Ends Soon!" It's getting so that you can put anyone's ad with someone else's headline, and lose nothing in the translation. How credible are your headlines, advertisements, and sales strategies? Are they the same overworked, overused phrases that everybody else uses, or do you really have a unique offer with special inventory to entice people to come in?

There's a furniture store in our town that has a sale every single week. Nonstop. Nothing's ever at a regular price. It's always the "biggest sale ever," "incredible savings," "everything's reduced!" I'm waiting to see the weekend when they run an ad that says, "We're not having a sale this weekend!" That would be a surprise. And since that has never happened, the New York State Attorney General took a dim view of their business practices and fined them tens of thousands of dollars for inflating mark-ups, then marking them down to fictitious sale prices.

American Family Publishers is ready to be tarred and feathered. Ed McMahon and Dick Clark have been telling the people who open their phony-baloney mailers that "If your name is drawn, YOU HAVE WON $10 MILLION! Check here if you want it in cash or certified check." Of course, the words "If your name is drawn" are so small that you'd need a 30-power magnifying glass to read them.

But the American public is catching on. And so is the FTC, the state attorneys general, the Federal courts, and the truth-in-advertising people. You can only fool your customers for so long. After a while it will destroy your business.

Credibility can be your biggest asset. It doesn't show on your financial statement. You can't write checks on it. But it might determine whether you're still selling instruments next week, next month, and in the years to come. Before you run your next sale, ask yourself if you're trying to fool your customers, or if you're just fooling yourself. Don't think about whether it will get past the Better Business Bureau. Think about how your customers will feel if they think they were suckered into buying an instrument through a false pretense, exaggerated claim, or some type of misrepresentation.

Just thumbing through last Sunday's paper, I saw the following sales statements:

Save $1,000 (on a $6,000 computer system). "Save" was so small it looked like the entire system was supposed to be $1,000. It wasn't. I'm sure the people who thought they were going to buy a system for $1,000 were pretty ticked off.

Prices are so low, we can't advertise them. It would only disrupt the pricing structure of the other dealers in the area. And if you believe that one, how about: Sale prices good this weekend only! These prices will never be this low again! Maybe on Monday they will be even lower. But don't tell their customers; they'll just have to have another sale.

We sell at wholesale, below cost, and below everybody! Just how do you think they make money to stay in business?

And the BS goes on and on. Doesn't make any difference if it's a car dealer, furniture store, music retailer, or electronics dealer. On the other hand, the fallout from the mega-sale merchants has gotten exceedingly high. Stores fail because they don't live up to their promises. When your credibility goes, you go too. It's a fact of life.

Dick Clark and Ed McMahon are learning through lawsuits. Local businesses learn by customers getting ticked and telling all their friends. The negative word-of-mouth advertising resulting from a phony sale can be disastrous. The sale might be a short-term answer, but you'll have a long-term problem.

There's an easy answer. Next time you run an incredible, fantastic, last chance, or you'll never see it again sale, you don't need to run it by the Better Business Bureau or your local lawyer. Just ask yourself, "Is it the truth?" If it is, you have nothing to worry about. But if it has even the smallest hint of deceit, you might be buying yourself a lawsuit, a loss of business, irritated customers, and sleepless nights.

Don't be a victim of "First I'll get money, then I'll get integrity." Just stick to some genuine truth-in-advertising elements. And think how good you'll feel when you're still in the music business years from now.

SELF-ANALYSIS

Check out the following list. How many of these things depict your store the way it is today? How many of these things did you do at one time, but stopped? It's important to periodically stop and take a look at your business through the eyes of a customer.

Self-Analysis

How do you stack up? Answer yes or no to the following statements.

❏ Yes   ❏ No   I am easy for clients to get a hold of. I have an answering machine and cell phone for times when no one is in the office.

Today you have to be available for clients who juggle full-time jobs and less free time. You have to cater to the customers' hours ... even weeknights and Sundays if necessary. If you don't, someone else could acquire your prospects and customers.

❏ Yes   ❏ No   My store is in an easy-to-find and convenient location.

Is it easy to give directions to your store? If not, you may be losing clients along the way to your location. If people can't figure out where your store is or how to get to it, they'll go somewhere they can find.

❏ Yes   ❏ No   Our store is neat and clean, and we have someone who checks to make sure it is spotless every day.

A messy office and dusty displays contradict the image you want to give to your customers, and take away from the value of your service.

❏ Yes   ❏ No   We offer a meaningful guarantee that addresses consumers' true concerns and puts our reputation on the line, every time.

Standing behind your work to the nth degree will separate you from the competition and make customers want to refer others to you. Doing expert work will assure that you will rarely be taken up on your guarantees. But having guarantees shows that you are responsible.

❏ Yes   ❏ No   Everyone on my staff is well-trained, and we provide training on an ongoing basis.

When you're green you're growing; when you're ripe you rot. You need ongoing learning on a regular basis to keep your staff up-to-date on the latest trends and techniques in the industry. Your employees aren't much help to customers if they are unaware of the latest music, or how to use the latest instruments. Your customers want to know that your employees are on the cutting edge, and that they can rely on them for up-to-date advice.

❏ Yes   ❏ No   I write my home phone number on the back of my business card when giving one to a prospect.

You want your customers to know that you are always available for them. Don't have your home phone number printed on the cards, or write it on ahead of time. The gesture has more power if you write it on the card in front of the prospect.

❏ Yes   ❏ No   I make it easy for customers to buy.

Customers are more likely to buy when you make it easy for them to afford to do so. Some people are uncomfortable paying a large amount of cash up front. Are checks OK? Do you accept credit cards?

❏ Yes   ❏ No   All of my employees are appropriately dressed.

What would you think if your doctor came into the examining room wearing a T-shirt with the name of a rock group on it, ripped jeans, and tennis shoes? Even if he had a degree from Harvard Medical School, you'd probably have doubts about everything he said to you. No matter how qualified your staff may be, prospects won't take them seriously unless they look professional.

❏ Yes   ❏ No   We pride ourselves on the way we handle incoming calls, and realize they are our greatest source of leads, new business, and customer satisfaction.

Every incoming call is an opportunity to make a new customer. When an employee answers your phone, he or she is quarterbacking your entire company.

❏ Yes   ❏ No   I read all of the trade magazines.

In order to serve your customers, you and your employees have to be up-to-date on the latest trends, developments, and equipment in the field. Many of your customers will have done some research before meeting you. It doesn't help your employees if they know less than the customers do. Subscribe to all of the trade magazines and keep them at the office for your employees to read.

❏ Yes   ❏ No   We have a newsletter that we send out to all of our customers and prospects at least quarterly.

Unlike some direct mail, newsletters will usually at least get looked at before they're thrown away. A newsletter gives you another contact with customers and prospects, and keeps your name out there. It's your opportunity to highlight new products, spotlight your employee-of-the-month and provide useful information.

❏ Yes   ❏ No   We always keep our promises.

If you don't, you'll have a difficult time increasing your business any time soon. Doing what you say you will shows integrity. Not doing what you say you will do shows carelessness or worse.

❏ Yes   ❏ No   We always try to find ways to make our business look different.

What are one or two things that make you stand out from the other music stores in town?

❏ Yes   ❏ No   We keep in touch with our loyal clients regularly with thank-you notes, customer appreciation days, holiday cards, and private open house events.

It costs five times as much to find new customers as it does to keep existing customers. It's easier and more cost-effective to keep your current customers happy than to court new ones. Current customers are the best source of new referrals and more business. Make them feel valued—reward them for doing business with you.

❏ Yes   ❏ No   We provide an e-mail address.

It may not be that important, but having an e-mail address shows that you are aware of current technology and that you are completely accessible.

❏ Yes   ❏ No   Our invoices and contracts are all clear, easy-to-read, and use very simple language.

Long, complex agreements make many customers uncomfortable. You don't want to slow the selling process or compromise the good feelings that have built up during the process by using a complicated contract or invoice.

❏ Yes   ❏ No   We try to make every client feel special, like each one is the most important we have.

Personality skills are important in catering to a customer's wants and needs. When a salesperson is with a customer, that customer should be the focus of his or her attention—everything else can wait.

❏ Yes   ❏ No   We always try to do something extra for the customer.

Go out of your way to keep customers happy; you never know how many friends they may refer to you in the future. If a customer requests a product you don't currently own, go ahead and get it. The goodwill that results will be worth more than the few dollars it costs you.

How many of the preceding statements could you honestly say "yes" to? How many of them struck a nerve, and remind you that, with a little ingenuity and creativeness, you could increase your business right away? If you are saying "no" to more than three, you might want to reassess your customer service thoughts and goals.

In today's business world, customers demand and get the service that they pay for. Most customers who get poor service never do business with that company again. And they tell all of their friends to avoid it as well. But those who have a positive experience, not only keep coming back for more, they send their friends to the store, too.

Keep in mind that the Golden Rule has to be modified if you really want to crank your sales up a notch. The Golden Rule is: "Do unto others as you would have them do unto you." You need to follow the Platinum Rule: "Do unto others as they want to be done unto." Customer service requires you to give your customers what they want, if you want them to keep coming back.

Five Little Things You Can Do to Win Customers

There are hundreds (if not thousands) of things you can do to win over customers. Some are creative, some are costly, and some are just plain clever. If you're looking for creative and clever without any significant cost, here are five things you might want to consider:

1) Print business cards for every employee. I did a whole book on this. Business cards are so cheap that everyone who works in your store (even part-time) should have them. Make up clever titles. Get your people to hand one out after every sale with a number to call in case of a question or problem. People are proud of their business cards, and you'll find they'll give them to their relatives and friends and other people they meet. That gets the name of your store out there and when someone thinks about buying a musical instrument, the name of your store might be in the front of their brain.

2) Never let the customer feel stupid. At one time or another you may have gone into an electronics store with a gadget that refused to work, only to find that you just didn't read the directions correctly, or you had the batteries in backwards. Then the clerk pointed out your stupidity and you felt like a second-rate citizen, and you hoped that no one in the store saw your embarrassment. When someone comes into your store expecting an unreasonable price or they have a question that a 3rd grader could have answered, just put yourself in their shoes and treat them like you would like to be treated. Talking down to them or embarrassing them might make you feel good for a few seconds, but you'll take the chance of losing a customer, who will then tell all their friends how badly they were treated.

3) Win over the entire family. Sometimes a whole family comes in even though only one person is in the market for an instrument. Coloring books and crayons can occupy the little ones, or having a special section of your store where they can sit and watch cartoons can be a big help. Soft drinks can make you a hero. If they're carrying a little dog and you've got a bag of dog biscuits in the back room, you can be an instant friend. Making your store family-friendly will get people to come back to you over and over.

4) Make sure you have an after-hours answering machine for inquiries and complaints. Check it once in awhile after the store is closed. More importantly, make sure your message states when someone will call back. It could be the start of the next business day, or even before … just let them know so they don't wonder when their call will be returned.

5) Reach out and touch them. This is the biggest thing you can do to win over customers and keep them coming back. It's also the hardest to get your salespeople to do. Every day have your salespeople (when they're not busy) call six previous customers for three things: 1. To find out if they're happy and to correct any problems; 2. To tell your customers about upcoming events, new products, special sales, or to come in again to do business with you for the rest of their lives; 3. To tell the customers to tell their friends about you because that's how you earn your living and you would like to make other people happy as well.

Think about #5 again. If you have three salespeople calling six people per day, five days a week, that's 90 calls a week. That's 4,680 calls a year. Wow, if just a small portion of those people came back in, think of how many more sales you'll make. It doesn't matter when you call. If the people you call are not home, just leave a message that you have "good news for them," and ask them to call you back. They will. People love good news. You can tell them about upcoming events—clinics, concerts, sales, and all the other good stuff going on in your store.

These are five little things that you can implement for a proactive marketing program that you can do right away without costing a bunch of money. No matter how clever your next advertising campaign is, or how aggressive your marketing efforts are, most people's impressions of your store will be by the little things you do. This gets people talking about you, and positive word-of-mouth promotion can keep you miles ahead of your competition.

Achieving Your Goal

So, here are some ideas for achieving whatever your goals may be:

1) Whatever your goal is, write it down. Anytime an idea pops into your head, write it down. If you see it on paper, it will make more sense and become more realistic and easier to achieve.

2) Make sure you have the intention to go after it. Intentions precede actions. If you don't intend to go after your goal, why bother to have it to begin with? Desire is a tremendous factor in achieving your goals

3) You need persistence and the patience to achieve what you want. Not giving up falls in here somewhere. Sometimes it means shifting gears, changing your plan of action, or coming up with a different set of ideas.

4) If you want something bad enough, you will always find a way to get it. I don't care what it is. Maybe it's to own your own jet, learn a second language, be the mayor of your town, or retire at an early age. No matter how far-fetched any goal may be, it's attainable if you want it bad enough. And that might require giving up something … maybe a lot of something.

5) Here's the kicker for achieving goals—passion. You have to really love what you do, and that's where people in the music business have the edge. We love what we do. It's fun. It's exciting. There's nothing like being in our business.

So, let's write down a couple of goals right now. See if you really intend to go after them, or are just giving them lip service. See if you have the persistence and drive to get what you're after. And then ask yourself how bad you want to achieve them. You might be surprised at what the answer is. And if you want to reach your goals bad enough, you'll achieve them.

Common goals:
- Create a stronger Internet presence
- Increase your lesson programs
- Take on a new line of products
- Open an additional store
- Renovate your store

What are your goals?

_____

_____

_____

_____

How will you achieve your goal?

_____

_____

_____

_____

_____

_____

What risks might you have to face?

_____

_____

_____

_____

_____

_____

Now, no excuses. Go for your goal!

Putting Together a Game Plan

Creating your own leads starts with having a game plan that you can follow each day. If you call three current customers who have already bought, three prospects who came in your store but didn't buy, and three total strangers, you'll be making nine calls a day or approximately 200 calls per month. If you make a new sale to only 10% of these people, that's an extra 20 units per month! The first way to get started is by talking to a certain number of people each day who are current customers. Give them a call.

Remember:

- See if they have any questions that you might be able to answer.
- See if they're happy.
- Find out if anyone else they know might be interested in an instrument.

These are leads by referrals. One satisfied customer can get you two more. All you've got to explain is that you get a lot of business from customers who are happy with their instruments, just like they are. And by the way, do they know of anyone else who might be interested in that particular instrument? You can put it in your own words. Find out what works for you and capitalize on it.

Start a list here of previous customers who you can look to for referrals:

_____

_____

_____

_____

You can generate a lot of leads through outside exposure: mall shows, home shows, warehouse club promotions, state and county fairs, and so on. Make a list of the consumer events in your area that you can attend.

_____

_____

_____

_____

_____

Your leads are also going to come from store advertising, in-store concerts, and various promotions run throughout the year. So, who do you know? Here is a list of memory joggers:

Who is your barber?	Who was at your wedding?
Who sold you your car?	Who is your veterinarian?
Who took your family photos?	Who sold you your wedding ring?
Who sells you suits?	Who is your nurse?
Who do rents your home?	Who do you know from an old job?
Who went to college with you?	Who owns a grocery store?
Who is in your old neighborhood?	Who do your children know?
Who is on your Christmas list?	Who is your florist?
Who is in your lodge or club?	Who is your painter/decorator?
Who lives next door?	Who do you play golf with?
Who do you write checks to?	Who send you e-mail?

Think about the people in your center of influence who might be prospects of a referral source. Add them here:

_____

_____

_____

_____

_____

You never know where your next customer may be coming from! Everyone you run into each day is a potential new customer. They may soon be in the market for an instrument. Or they may know someone who is and pass on your name. You can't just wait around for walk-ins; you have to bring in new customers.

Does Your Music Store Have a Newsletter?

Here some topics you may want to cover in your monthly or quarterly newsletter:

- Items that are on sale
- Coupons to bring to the store
- Tips for playing a particular instrument
- Instrument cleaning tips
- Schedule of concerts in the area
- Lessons schedule for your store
- Feature a customer that shops in your store; why they love music
- Feature local celebrities who shop in the store or use a product
- Introduce your staff: an employee of the month or quarter
- A letter from you, the owner
- News about customers' accomplishments
- List of customer recitals
- Updates and renovations to the store
- New products
- Store contest or raffle winners

Think about breaking the newsletter into sections:

- Products
- People
- Events
- Deals
- Playing

Think about all the current and potential customers you can reach by sending out this newsletter. Send it to:

1) All past customers
2) All current customers
3) Some people at random from the phone book
4) A few people at random from the newspaper
5) People or businesses that you do business with outside of the store.

Call some to check in and see if they received the newsletter. Ask them what they thought and if they are in they are looking to buy.

A Personal Touch

Looking for an Opinion:

Calling people on the phone to try to get them in to buy an instrument can be difficult, especially if your prospect thinks that sale is the only intent of your call. Nobody wants to be sold anything; they want to *buy* it.

Remember:

- Think about the tone of your call.
- Talk about new models, or something that wasn't on your floor when the prospect came in before.
- People like to be asked their opinion.
- Offer them a thank-you gift.

Personal Visits:

Going to a person's home takes a lot of time and effort, but it can be extremely effective if you can get the instrument in the hands of your prospect in their own home.

Just having it on the truck is a good reason to stop by for a personal visit. The more times you personally talk to a prospect, the closer you'll be to a sale.

Who can you call or see to set up a home demo right away:

_____

_____

_____

_____

_____

Using the Phone

Cold Call Tips

- Be passionate. If you're excited about your products, your potential new customers will be too. Stand behind your business; people will be able to sense your enthusiasm.
- Be prepared. Who are you calling? How does what you are offering fit into their life? Do some research. Prepare for what you will say and imagine the call going well.
- Be yourself and be personal. People want you to stand out from the rest. It will get and keep their attention better. Try your best to develop an authentic relationship with the potential new customer.
- Be inquisitive. Don't just talk about the business. Ask them about themselves and their experience with music. Ask what they would be in the market for. If they are not interested then ask for referrals.
- Don't want to make too many calls in one day. More than a dozen in a row is a lot of calls. You can get burned out easily. Rejection is tough to take.

Remember:
- Make sure you have the proper environment when making follow-up phone calls.
- Don't follow up leads when you're in a rush.
- Start by calling a customer or two with whom you have great rapport; someone who's really happy with their current instrument.
- Don't sound like a salesperson. You want to sound like a friend.
- Start the conversation with something that will make them interested in talking with you. Don't start by saying, "How are you today?"

Write some ideas for opening lines here:

_____

_____

_____

_____

Leaving Messages

When you call your lead, the chances are only about 50% that you're going to reach them on the phone. Many people put their phone in the hands of an answering machine.

If you reach a machine, don't spill all your information in the hopes of getting a return call. Too much information and they don't need to talk to you. They might make a negative decision on their own and never call you back.

List ideas for leaving a message on a home answering machine:

_____

_____

_____

_____

Or try, "I've got some good news for you. Give me a call back."

When trying to reach someone at their office, you're likely to run into a receptionist or secretary whose function is to screen all calls and to decide if they should be put through.

List ideas of how to get past a person screening calls:

_____

_____

_____

_____

_____

_____

Using the Mail

Many times the best way to follow up a lead is through direct mail with telephone follow up, particularly if the prospect isn't that knowledgeable about the instrument you'll be discussing.

Remember:
- Try to stay away from using a postage meter.
- Handwrite the name and address.
- Consider using a personal-size envelope rather than legal size.
- Don't waste a lot of words on "fluff." Get to the point.

Postcards

If you're sending a postcard in the hopes of getting a prospect to come to the store, you might want to write a note in longhand saying:

_____

_____

_____

_____

_____

If you're dropping a line to a recent customer, you might want to write:

_____

_____

_____

_____

_____

Staying in touch with customers and prospects on a regular basis pays big dividends!

214   Bob Popyk

Bringing Them Back

If you're really serious about saving deals, creating more business for yourself, or simply bringing back a customer one more time, here are a couple ideas. Go visit a car dealership and test-drive a new car. See how the salesperson follows up afterward. Inquire about an insurance policy from an excellent insurance broker and see how he handles the lead. Go to an open house and see if the real estate agent calls you over the next few days. In other words, learn from others. Do they send you a note in the mail? Do they track you down at home or work? See what works and what is hopeless. Then blend the best ones into what will work for you. There are no bad ideas when trying to save a sale or trying to put a deal together (if they work), but some are definitely better than others.

See How Others Do It

- Car salesmen: Do they call you days later to inquire about your possible purchase?
- Insurance salesmen: Do they keep in touch and follow through?
- Real estate agents: Do they check back to see if you're interested?
- Even retail stores: Nordstrom, an upscale department store, is known for their customer service. They call customers, they send thank-you notes, and they follow up. They go above and beyond to gain and retain customers.

Take notes on their methods of "bringing them back."

_____

_____

_____

Sample Letter:

Watch out for your former customers in the newspaper. An engagement, marriage or career advancement may be the perfect opportunity to earn them back as customers. Use this sample letter to start:

Dear (Former Customer),

Congratulations on your _____. What an exciting step for you. We miss doing business you and would love the opportunity to see you again. Stop by the store for a free gift in celebration of your accomplishment. See you soon!

Sincerely, (Your Name)

12 Easy Ways to Keep Your Customers Loyal

I remember going into my local coffee house years and years ago. The owner was in the market for a new car, and one of the local car dealers came into his shop. He said to the owner, "I hope you buy a car from one of my dealerships here in the area. I stop in here for coffee every day, and I'd hate to see one of my competitor's cars in your parking space. If we want to see our village grow, we need to do business with each other." He was right. It's like a mutual admiration society. It's one of the better 12 ways to turn someone into a loyal customer. It's important to keep a customer coming back to you and having them refer their friends to you. Here are 12 customer loyalty ideas that are sometimes overlooked.

Customer Loyalty Checklist:

1) Helping promote your customer's products and services is one of the ways to keep customer loyalty in check. Letting them know you're using their products and services yourself, gives you an edge for their repeat business and their referrals.

What do some of your highest spending customers do? How can you show them that you value what they do? See if they return the favor.

2) Keep in touch with them. Send them a thank-you note after a purchase. Call once in a while to let them know about a special sale, new product, or to see how they're doing. It's basic, and it works.

What other opportunities can you take to call customers, send them a note and get them to return to the store?

3) Return customer calls promptly. Since so many people don't return calls today, or hide behind voice mail, you are already at an advantage when you pick up the phone. If you are out of your place of business and can't return calls for a few days, convey that in your voice mail message with the promise to get back to the caller as quickly as possible. For e-mail, use an automatic response promising to get back to the person as soon as possible.

Example: "Thank you for calling ABC Music, the only store with XYZ! I am out of the office until Wednesday. Please leave me a message and I will be sure to return your call promptly upon my return!"

4) Under-promise and over-deliver. You've heard it before. If you haven't figured it out by now. Be careful with claims and exaggerations, and keep the hype to a minimum. Just find out what a customer wants and give it

to them, but with just a little bit more. That "little bit more" could simply be in the way of more attention, quicker service, or a pleasant attitude.

Don't forget: Remind your customer what they are getting for no charge. Include it on the invoice or receipt.

5) Be accessible. Be approachable. Make sure you are personally available and willing to help customers whenever there is a problem. Personal involvement can have a magic effect. If you're the owner of your business, decide how much of a starring role you're going to play. If you are working behind the scenes, have a point person in place who is willing to play the part.

6) Appearance counts. Keep your store looking up-to-date. Perception is reality, and the reality is that people do judge a book by its cover. Every so often take a look at your place of business from your customer's eyes. Would you enjoy coming into your store as a customer?

7) Give back to your customers. Offer your repeat customers special savings with a customer appreciation night, preferred customer sales, and a priority look at special events

8) Do things for your customer's convenience, not yours. Make it as easy as possible for customers to do business with you. The easier you can make it for customers, the more business you will have. Determine all the ways you can eliminate the hassle factor.

9) Send or give an invoice periodically with "no charge" on it. It could be for a service or a small accessory. This will help your customers remember you. And if it is unexpected, it will have a much larger impact.

10) Be kind. Your mother was right, be nice to people. Be careful and avoid getting into arguments with the customer, even when they're wrong. The customer isn't always right, but how you handle the situation makes all the difference.

11) Treat employees well. If they are treated poorly, there's a good chance they will take it out on your customers. Try to keep your staff happy. A smile with a customer can do wonders.

12) Don't show an attitude of indifference to customers. In a recent study on why people stop doing business with certain companies, 68% quit because of an attitude of indifference toward the customers by the owner, manager, or salesperson. Never treat a customer like they're an intrusion on your day, and make sure no one else in your store does either.

Think of customer loyalty like starting an airplane engine by hand. That first crank can be very hard, but once you get the prop spinning, it will continue on it's own. Never take it for granted that a customer will return. You have too much competition vying for their business. It's a fast-changing and competitive environment out there. Excellent customer service is essential for success. Make sure you're on top of it.

Other Books and DVDs by Bob Popyk

It's Up to You!

There are many excuses for why business may be off, sales might be slow, or customers may not be coming through your door. But as columnist and sales and marketing writer Bob Popyk points out it's up to you to find a way to increase business. This book offers a "best of Bob" collection of columns from 1990–1997, providing hundreds of ideas for elevating your music business.

How to Find Gigs That Pay Big Bucks

Is your talent still locked up in a garage? If so learn how to land the gigs that pay serious money from some of the music business premiere musicians, agents, promoters, and talent buyers. This video is for anyone who dreams of making a living as a musician with advice from rockers like Bon Jovi's Richie Sambora, Kevin Cronin of REO Speedwagon, Eric Schenkman of Spin Doctors, and Joe Satriani. Learn how to get gigs in casinos, cruise ships, and opening for headline acts. The video is available in DVD or VHS formats.

Here's My Card

Praised for its advice on marketing with a business card, Bob Popyk not only shows you why your business card is so important, but he also teaches you how to use it to create more business. Norm Poltenson of *The Business Journal* says "it's probably the very best book on business card networking ever written!" Available in paperback, this book is a perfect for anyone who's ever wanted to see their business cards do more than sit in someone's wallet.

The Business of Getting More Gigs

As a musician, you can't sit around waiting for the phone to ring, offering you the perfect gig. You have to have a plan; you need to network and constantly market yourself. In this collection of Bob Popyk columns from *International Musician*, the American Federation of Musicians official magazine, you'll learn how to land gigs that pay the bills. There are musicians out there who have a full calendar of work, no matter what month or season it is. Bob teaches you how to treat your music like a business and shares with you how to be clever, innovative, and the ultimate self-promoter.

Visit www.BobPopyk.com for more information or to order.